Sacred Journey of a

Celtic Visionary

Cover Photograph: Aðalsteinn Eyþórsson, Iceland

Cover, graphics and layout by Davin Larkin
www.davinlarkin.com

Note for Librarians: A cataloguing record for this book is available from Library and Archives Canada at www.collectionscanada.ca/amicus/index-e.html
ISBN 1-4251-0975-6

Printed in Victoria, BC, Canada. Printed on paper with minimum 30% recycled fibre.
Trafford's print shop runs on "green energy" from solar, wind and other environmentally-friendly power sources.

TRAFFORD
PUBLISHING™

Offices in Canada, USA, Ireland and UK

Book sales for North America and international:
Trafford Publishing, 6E–2333 Government St.,
Victoria, BC V8T 4P4 CANADA
phone 250 383 6864 (toll-free 1 888 232 4444)
fax 250 383 6804; email to orders@trafford.com
Book sales in Europe:
Trafford Publishing (UK) Limited, 9 Park End Street, 2nd Floor
Oxford, UK OX1 1HH UNITED KINGDOM
phone +44 (0)1865 722 113 (local rate 0845 230 9601)
facsimile +44 (0)1865 722 868; info.uk@trafford.com
Order online at:
trafford.com/06-2734

10 9 8 7 6 5 4 3 2

Sacred Journey of a Celtic Visionary

Tricia Sheehan

White Feather Healing

TRAFFORD
PUBLISHING™

Biography

Tricia Sheehan was born on 9th. March 1956, on the west coast of Ireland, and after being resident there for two and a half years, her family moved to live in the suburbs of Dublin, where she was reared. After secondary school, she attended commercial college for a year and subsequently studied accounting. At twenty two she married and gave birth to her two sons.

In her late twenties she began to study in the arena of spiritual healing and personal development and became a 'probationer member' of the National Federation of Spiritual Healers (NFSH) in Great Britain. Some years and much study later she became a full healing member of the NFSH. Her healing career has evolved and developed over the last twenty years encompassing both individual and group work and stress management workshops for the corporate sector.

Her work and study now, focuses on the 'cellular memory patterns' of an individual, looking at the underlying attitude patterns, emotional challenges, past lifetime imprints, spiritual dreams and whatever encompasses that individual, interpreting what she sees and guiding the person, to give birth to their dreams or heal whatever issues they are dealing with. She looks to the core of an individual, to see what is really happening on a spiritual/emotional or physical level and then creates a personal meditative healing journey on tape for them.

She now lives and works in Co. Meath close to family and friends. Her home however is on the road to the West, where she continues to travel to work and breathe the air of the Atlantic Ocean that gave birth to her journey. She is currently working on her second book, an exploration of 'Cellular Memory Patterns' and how to use them as a vital tool for learning, growth and personal development.

Contact Tricia

www.whitefeatherhealing.com
info@whitefeatherhealing.com

Dedication

For Anne
A personal physician
and
sacred magician
Thank you for everything

Acknowledgments

Firstly, thank you Mam and Dad for everything. My flavour and scent would not be quite the same this lifetime, without you.

Linda, you have stood behind me, encouraging, supporting and believing in me and my work. You truly are the midwife of this book. I am deeply grateful to you.

Davin, my baby and gifted son, for the graphics, artwork and so much more - I thank you for your expertise, time and huge dedication to me and my book.

Thank you Anne, for listening endlessly to 'my voice', for proofreading, editing and the nourishment necessary to sustain me through this journey.

In those final days, when I could no longer spell or read, thank you Rachel, my godchild, for coming to my rescue.

Due to the early departure of 'my parents' from this Earth,

I am especially grateful to my sister and sister-in-law, Marian and Pauline, my brothers Eanna and Barry and all my yummy nieces and handsome nephew, for loving me 'just the way I am'.

Thank you to my precious worldly wise firstborn son Kenn and his Celine, for my beautiful grandchildren, Ella and Cian and Richelle and of course Katie and Nikki.

A huge thank you goes to my ancestors, who gifted me all that I stepped into when I entered this World.

Thank you Gerry for supporting my work and saying yes to its publication - you have been a precious part of my journey.

Thank you Caitriona, Joan and all those who agreed to have our shared stories included.

Indi, my guides, angels and soul family – thank you for your guidance, divine inspiration and heavenly wisdom and for holding me at times when I am unable to walk.

Thank you – thank you, my precious and wonderful friends. You know who you are. I would be lost without you.

I am hugely grateful to those clients that very kindly wrote their stories, for inclusion in this book. I am blessed to know you.

Thank you to my teachers and all those who have sculpted my journey using the tools of love, compassion and wisdom.

And 'Trafford Publishing' – where would I be without you? You have made it possible and affordable for me to publish 'my dream' and to give birth to 'my baby'. Thank you Noeleen in the 'Irish office', for your warmth, expertise and prompt answers to my questions.

Thank you to all those who have walked the journey with me-I am deeply grateful to you.

Finally, the deepest gratitude goes to 'my inner child' as without your bravery and courage, I or this book would not be. You are my first breath.

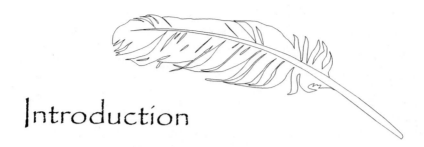

Introduction

Every life lived is a story waiting to be told. This is the story of a life that captures vividly the journey from the womb into the multi-dimensional world we all inhabit. With simple truth and vision, we see through the eyes of 'White Feather', all the intricate webs we weave, as we experience birth and all the challenges of Living.

This story evokes the essence of the people and the events that shaped this journey. The writing draws you into the heart of the story and awakens your senses, so that there is no veil separating you, from the experiences unfolding on each page. As the story unfolds, so also does the bigger picture, illustrating the spiritual and emotional patterns that underscore the choices made, the relationships born, the births, deaths and all the twists and turns that directed the course of this journey.

This story stands on the shoulders of the wild rocky slopes of Cape Clear Island and the smooth grey windswept limestone coastline of the Burren and all such places that endure on this Earth. Their presence reminds us that life endures, our stories endure and the impact we make on each other and this Earth endures. In a world where life has become so disposable, it is a good thing to sit on these ancient shoulders and read a story of heart, spirit and hope.

It is refreshing to read a story that belongs to all of us, providing an insight into patterns and stories which our bodies, our relationships and our apparent random choices hold. This story sculpts a bridge between a generation that had no language, to give life to its emotional and spiritual roots and the evolving generations, struggling to come to terms with the unearthing of those same roots. 'White Feather' shines a soft and revealing light on the deep currents that catch all of us who make this journey and in doing so, she brings hope and understanding and a touch of magic, to ease the way.

Anne Campbell

A Fresh Start

Sat 10th Sept, 05   (Matala, South Crete)

Our journey to Crete began Saturday 3rd. September. Our luggage never arrived. It was lost somewhere in transit. A week later it is still missing! There have been sightings in Dublin, London and Athens but lo and behold, it has given them the slip, yet again.

Since I arrived, despite my nakedness, my eyes have been drawn towards the skies, where I have observed eagles, in ones and twos, soaring at great heights and somehow, I feel guided on this journey, by these sacred messengers, whom I have never observed, before now.

This last eighteen months for me, has been a challenging time and I know I am being spiritually initiated, into the next phase of the journey; the birth of this book. It makes sense of the huge emotional clearing I am experiencing. This time too will pass I remind myself, and the miracle of birth, makes the labour worthwhile, as anyone who has given birth to a project or child will know.

Last night I dreamt, I saw an eagle soar and gliding expertly, it landed on the ground close to me. I was fascinated by the eagle, but as it fixed its eyes on me and began to follow me, I felt very frightened and ran to hide somewhere. I then woke up, hearing clearly in my mind "the eagle has landed".

The eagle soars to the highest point in the skies and with accurate precision, sees every aspect of what is beneath, even the tiniest movement. The eagle represents the birth of this book, that I have begun writing today, the telling of my story, the sharing of all the wisdom I have gathered and the awareness that has awoken in me over time.

As with every precious project there is fear – the fear of exposure, judgement or abandonment. Yet, I know, I am more than ready to write this book and to gift all that I am creatively to the Earth. And so the story begins..............

Chapter 1

Birth and Beginnings

My fantasy is that I rode on the back of a powerful whale, from the deepest ocean, swimming through the giant red waves of the Atlantic and birthed onto the shores of the Burren in Co. Clare, Western Ireland.

In reality on 9th March 1956, my mother was haemorrhaging and had to make the terrifying trip by car, some forty miles, from the Burren on one side of the bay to Galway city on the other. She must have been very scared that she would not survive. We arrived in Calvary Hospital (aptly named), Galway and in her words, a doctor who treated her like a butcher took over, breaking her waters and spraying the walls with her blood. We were, both of us, in grave danger. It was my first near death experience but we survived and here I am to tell my tale.

My mother born Bridget, but called Brid, was young, just

twenty three when I was born. She was dark haired and very beautiful. I was her second child. My sister Marian was born two years and three months earlier.

My mother was reared on the foothills of the Burren, on the edge of the Atlantic Ocean that looks across to Galway bay and the Aran islands. It is a wild and beautiful place, the unique lunar landscape, home to many species of wildflowers and animals and the stone mountains seen from space have a great similarity to the moon. As always, the ocean there has many faces, most often pounding the coastline with big waves, but every now and then, calmness and stillness descends, as if the ocean were playing a lullaby, to a sleeping baby. My mother was one of nine children and her parents Delia and Joe MacNamara, ran a business, which consisted of a grocery shop, flour and grain store, farmlands and later a petrol station. They were hardworking and wealthy for their time.

My mother met my father, Michael Sheehan, some 18 years her senior, when she was around 17 or 18. He was the principal of a small primary school in Ballyvaughan, Co. Clare. He was a handsome, kind, hardworking man, very dedicated to his wife, children and career. Both of my parents were born in August, under the astrological sign of Leo. My father was born and reared on 'Oilean Chleire', an Irish speaking island, the most southerly island in west Cork, southern Ireland. It is a stunningly beautiful wild mountainous island, with views to the famous Fastnet lighthouse (of yachting fame) and onwards to the U.S.A. The winters there are harsh and often in those days, storms would cut off the inhabitants from the mainland for a substantial period. My father was one of the eldest of ten children and as his father, Tommie, spent many months away at sea, fishing each year, my father helped his mother Catherine to rear the younger children. They were very poor being barefoot for a lot of their childhood, yet my father spoke of storytelling, dancing and music and had a deep love of his home place. While having a deep desire to become a fisherman, my father was very clever at school, winning a scholarship to be schooled in a boarding school in Dublin and later another scholarship to a training college in Waterford, south east Ireland to train as a primary school teacher, so fishing became a hobby rather than a career. Following the footprints of his career, led him to Co. Clare, where he met, fell in love with and married my mother. We lived in a rented cottage, on the edge of the ocean in Ballyvaughan, Co. Clare.

My mother said I screamed solidly for six months, after I was born (what a nightmare!) and had to be fed baby food for problem children. However, I shut up after that six month period (for a number of years at any rate) and she said I became the quietest of her four children.

My quest to free my soul and spirit, to express all that I am, through my physical and emotional body, is reflected in the wild beautiful places my parents hailed from. Also, the Burren, akin to the moon (the moon representing the emotional mother of the Earth), reflected the huge journey of emotional development, healing and teaching I was to take.

When later at twenty seven, I embarked on a spiritual and emotional journey of discovery about myself, I was regressed, through a meditative journey, back to my birth and I felt so intensely guilty and responsible for hurting my mother and causing her the pain of my birth, that I carried with me a sense of deep unworthiness and a need to make up for it, for many years. I felt that no matter what I did, it was never good enough for her. The circumstances of my birth awakened old attitude patterns in me (from past lifetimes I believe), that I brought into this life, to be healed and also created a difficult relationship with my mother, for that first six months and again as a teenager, one we would heal, much later on.

During that birth regression, and the exploration of the near death experience, I realised a part of me wanted to go back into the spirit world, as I was terrified of my deep sensitivity and the journey ahead, but another part of me was rock solid and determined to stay with the plan. We come to this Earth, with a spiritual scroll, wherein is written, all that we desire to learn, explore, express and experience in a given lifetime. This contract or scroll is written by our creative spiritual selves, and so we have a definite journey in mind, when we enter the Earth. It is my understanding, that we choose our parents, surroundings and the circumstances of our birth, so there is no random chance. It is a well crafted choice we make.

We are individuals with free will, a will no one but us can control, and when others appear to control us, it is only because we are allowing them to do so for a period, because we have de-activated our own 'free will' for some reason or other. Having said that, spiritually we often choose very challenging circumstances to learn and grow through and we deserve an abundance of love and support to encourage us through. We have to honour the chosen journeys of others and support them in whatever way is comfortable for us.

So, getting back to my birth, I did some healing and transformational work, (at age thirty) which I will explain later and it greatly relieved the pressure of that time. A side effect of the circumstances of my birth, was that I experienced terror of death or serious illness and also a sense of becoming 'spaced out' and that I was leaving my body, many times, when I drove long journeys in the car alone. It took me a while to recognise that stored in my cells, was the memory of my mother and I panicking that we would not survive, at the time of my birth, thus the car journeys on my own, activated that memory. My mother and I must have felt very alone and scared during that journey. So, I have journeyed into my cells many times, to heal this memory and now I find long journeys alone in the car a much more comfortable experience. Our cells store and remember everything about us, all of our experiences, emotions, reactions and sensations. All things can be transformed and healed within us and yes only we can heal ourselves, but all the support, therapy and encouragement we need, is there for us, from the heavens and the earth, once we reach out for it. So, if you need support, reach out and ask for it, that's why it is there.

We are interconnected in this web of life, all needing the support and wisdom of the other.

Co. Clare gifted me my loving parents, grandparents, sister, family, friends and the powerful ocean, whose breath is in every cell of my body. I am a Piscean, a water creature, birthed onto the land and the wild free energy of the Burren in Co. Clare, western Ireland.

Chapter 2

East meets West

When I was at the tender age of two and a half, my parents decided to leave the West and journey to put their roots down in the East of Ireland. As I write the word East, it feels alien to my western birthplace. They chose a home in the developing suburbs of west Dublin, and my father secured a teaching position, in a very large school which he was later to become principal of. I promptly became very ill, with what was diagnosed as gastro enteritis. My mother set up a makeshift bed, in our new breakfast room, just beside the kitchen and patiently put teaspoons of fluid into my mouth, to try and keep me hydrated, but my condition deteriorated. In a state of near unconsciousness, I was moved to hospital, where I was placed in an oxygen tent. At that time, parents were not allowed to stay and visits were brief, so not alone had I been taken away from my beloved grandmother, relations, friends and wild western ocean, now I was also separated from my parents and sister.

Having been snatched from the cradle of western Ireland and all that it contained, and from the familiar loving arms of my parents, I wanted to die and experienced the second near death experience, of my short life. Later I regressed back to that time, and saw that leaving my grandmother, Mam-a-Mac, as we called her, had a dramatic effect on me. She had a similar sensitivity to me, and she was the only adult female around me, at that time, who felt like a kindred spirit. I grieved hugely for that time, when I was much older. During that regression, I felt very scared without my grandmother and again, that I wanted to return to the spirit world, as I felt terrified of my sensitivity and difference, and had a huge fear that I would not survive or be nurtured in this World. Again, there was a solid part of me (stubborn some might say) that was staying with the job, and so I recovered. I know heaven and my guides and angels as well as the doctors and nurses were working hard to support me in the recovery process, at that time. Gastro enteritis effects the tummy area, and this area governs a persons self worth, self belief and ability to function with confidence and be nurtured in the Earth, and I carried huge fears, that resulted from painful past life experiences, into the Earth with me, to be healed, in this regard.

Our lives settled into a pattern, and I settled down. I loved Primary school and had a wonderful teacher, called Mrs. Fleming, throughout most of my primary education. She was not formally trained, but was a naturally gifted and very brilliant teacher and I flourished, proudly wearing the metallic green captain's badge (given for top marks in the class) every other week. My mother said I would not eat, until I had completed my homework, underneath the table, the moment I returned from school. I loved learning, reading and playing a myriad of games on the road with my friends.

Christmas and birthdays were very special times, in our home. My mother was very strict and disciplined, but it did not affect me unduly, at an early age, as I was a quiet child and tried very hard to please. She was also a wonderful homemaker, a great cook and a very brilliant seamstress. She made a lot of our clothes, hand smocking our dresses, when we were little. Christmas day was magical. It began with seven a.m. Roman Catholic mass and Santa's room was always locked and out of bounds, until after mass. There was always something magical under the tree, a doll, books, games, a three wheeler bike once. Breakfast followed, always fresh grapefruit and a full Irish breakfast with homemade brown bread and 'old time Irish' marmalade. It was expected in our house, if my mother cooked, that we washed up and cleared the table. My father took an active role in running the home, when he was there. He nurtured my mother beautifully, as I observed it, putting a hot water bottle in her bed, making her coffee, cooking, cleaning and generally supporting her in every way he could. He always fed us, during the night, as babes and though he was teaching full time, he never allowed my mother to get up.

There were two rooms in our house, considered the good rooms, they being the dining room and sitting room, the latter being used for visits akin to that of the Pope!!!!!!! On

Christmas day, at two or three p.m., we descended on the 'dining room', sitting at the good table, that was adorned with a white linen tablecloth, the good china with the swans, silver cutlery that had been painstakingly cleaned, Christmas crackers and so forth. The china covered dishes, filled with perfectly cooked and buttered mashed potato, brussel sprouts and carrots arrived. Next came, the china sauce boat, filled with hot cranberry sauce and the piping hot china plates, adorned with perfectly cooked turkey, ham and divine bread stuffing. It was followed by homemade plum pudding, (always set alight in the darkness, to our great delight as children), with brandy sauce, sherry trifle and Christmas cake. The crackers, hats, jokes and a cup of tea followed, accompanied by the circus on the television, and a lot of delicious over full moaning and groaning. This feast and the using of the 'good china' happened about once a year, and so Christmas day had a magical, out of the ordinary feel to it. It was only later, as a parent, that I realised, the hard work it took, to gift this type of day to ones children.

I always felt special on my birthday, receiving a card, a gift and a birthday cake and to this day, I celebrate myself on my birthday and have encouraged many friends, who disliked their birthdays, to do the same. When a child is born, we celebrate the miracle of birth and why not continue, honouring the preciousness of that child, throughout its lifetime.

During primary school, I had a lot of septic throats, had to be confined to bed regularly and often injected each day by the doctor. Eventually I was taken to a throat specialist, who decided to wait and see if I would grow out of it. Much later, I discovered that the throat area, governs expression and communication and as I opened my throat area, to give a voice to my inner feelings and dreams, my throat responded and got fully better, so throat infections are not a problem for me any more.

We spent our summers, July and August of each year, in the west of Ireland, and I loved it. We rented an old house, called 'the residence', together with my Aunt Carmel's family, and there we bathed in the magic of the west, every summer holiday. My Dad spent many hours fishing with us, on the high rocks, overlooking the Atlantic Ocean and he held us, while we cast the rod, and taught us to sit, be still and guard the fish he caught, that jumped in the rock pools. He brought us to the sand hills, to swim, play and dig for sand eels that were used for fishing bait. He brought us to the Rock Mountains and taught us about the wild flowers. We walked to our grandparent's home, helped in the shop, popped sweets and chocolate into our mouths, served petrol and helped with gathering the hay for the winter months, and we were surrounded by aunts, uncles and cousins.

During one of our summers in Co. Clare, we went to visit my godparents in Ennis; Mary, my mother's sister and Jimmy her husband. They lived in a market town, where they had a three storey house, the ground floor was a supermarket and the upper floors their home. I was about eight or nine and wandered upstairs, where I met this old man, who in hindsight, looked like my uncle Jimmy, and we chatted for a while. He was sitting in one of the bedrooms. I thought nothing of it, till I mentioned to the adults, that I was talking to the man upstairs. They told me there was no man there, and I silently could not understand why they were lying to me. Repeatedly I asked about this man, but no one was ever willing to discuss it with me.

Astrologically, they say Piscean children are very psychic and can meet their granny on the stairs, but I guess many young children are open and psychic enabling them to have heightened spiritual experiences, like seeing people from the spirit world. This man, Jimmy's father was dead, but no one told me that either, at the time. Later, my son brought home some Co. Clare records and this man was listed as owning this home and having a business there. There was nothing extraordinary about chatting to him. It was the reaction, of the people around me that caught my attention.

One and a half years, after we moved to Dublin, my brother Finbarr (now known as Barry), was born prematurely. I adored my little brother and like all siblings, we played, laughed, fought and cried. As a toddler, he developed pneumonia and was taken to hospital, but twenty four hours, saw him bouncing back. My Mam told me to look at what happened to him, after all the fighting I had done with him. The cot was empty and at five or six, I felt so guilty and responsible, for making my little brother ill. We, as parents, have to be so careful with our children. I held the pain of that, for a long time.

When I was eight, my mother was confined to bed, with high blood pressure, as she was expecting my brother and the baby of our family, Eanna. My grandmother Mam-a-Mac died at that time. Dad took my sister Marian to the funeral and I stayed at home, with my Mam and brother Finbarr. We knelt around her bed and said rosaries (Catholic prayers). The house felt very sad and my Mam did not get to say goodbye to her Mother. We so need the ritual of saying goodbye. It is vital and supports the healing process. Many years later, I created a ritual to say goodbye to my beloved grandmother myself. A personal ritual can take many forms and one example is the writing of a letter to the person in spirit that you love and burying it in the garden while planting a new tree or shrub to celebrate that person.

Much later, as a young teenager in Clare, under the watchful eye of my spirit grandmother, I had my first 'french kiss', with a third or fourth cousin, called Peter. Being much more worldly wise and 'English', he had never heard the term 'french kiss', it was just how it was done. Tongues were a part of kissing and that was that. I, on the other hand, was a good Irish Catholic girl, and had a degree in cementing my lips firmly together and kissing like a seal, lest I commit a mortal sin, upset my parents, and be cast out of the house or into the burning fires of hell. However, I rose to the challenge, succumbed and it was divine. Thanks Peter – I have been doing it ever since. Teachers can arrive into our lives at any given moment and in the strangest of guises, so stay alert!

It is important to note here, that my parents were strict Catholics and expected us to adhere to the rules and regulations of the Catholic Church. We were afraid not to. This teaching is so fear based and controlling of a persons uniqueness and free will. However, there is a basic message of love and respect, that is vital to learn, in terms of how we treat ourselves and others, and this is the untainted gift of religious education. It was expected of us to go to confession, each week, make up some venial sins, do our penance, attend Mass and communion, kneel down and say the rosary, pray before bedtime, go to sodality, give up everything you love during Lent and attend all the Easter ceremonies.

A level of religion that is based on love and understanding, not criticism and sacrifice, is comforting for children and adults alike, but a deep seated teaching, of repetitive unworthiness, is very damaging. If I attend church now, for a funeral service, wedding or other ceremony, I change the 'unworthy' and 'sacrificial' words, in my mind, to ones of love and honour. All prayers need to be reviewed I guess, to honour, the spiritual, emotional, mental and physical growth, of this era in the Earth.

It was expected of us to know, we were unworthy weak human beings. Sex before marriage was a mortal sin, and could get you excommunicated (a fate worse than death). Pregnancy before marriage did not even have a sin bracket, so disgusting was it. One hid one's daughters, in a home somewhere and the adoption papers were signed, without question, and this was only thirty years ago. My Mother told me many times, that if I ever became pregnant before marriage, that I would be thrown out of the house, and she would have nothing more to do me, ever again, which left me terrified. I was scared, even kissing someone with my sealed lips, defying the danger of broken teeth from the pressure that sperm would sail from his body, through his clothing, through mine and into my body that was shut like a vault. Logic did not come into it, just sheer terror of my Mother and the church and being imperfect. The first time I told my beloved nieces these stories, they laughed till the tears rolled down their faces.

Before I move to the intensity of my teenage years, where all hell began to break loose, I want to tell you, about the wonderful trip, I took with my Father, to his home place – a one and only time, in my childhood, when I had him all to myself. I grew up, with my mother's people in Co. Clare, but my father's mother Catherine died before I was born and this trip was to be the one and only time I ever met, my paternal grandfather, Thomas Sheehan. As I write, I feel sad our time together, was so limited. My Dad and I made the long journey, of about five hours to the most southern part of Ireland, West Cork. We stayed for a night in the 'West Cork Hotel', in Skibberreen, (the only night I ever remember, spending in a hotel as a child), where my father knew the owner. The next day, we headed to Baltimore (one can go no further) and a fishing boat owned by a friend of my Dad's, took us the hours journey to 'Cape Clear Island', known as 'Oilean Chleire'. As it was my first trip on a boat, I stared in awe, at the ocean, all around me, and as I am just a land based whale, I felt right at home. I don't recall having visited the island previous to this. This trip felt like a series of firsts.

We walked up the very steep hill, of this beautiful unspoiled island, that smells of salt, sea, wild flowers and wonder, to my Dad's home place. Kennedy, the big sheepdog greeted us along with Uncle Joe, my Dad's brother, Julia his wife and the children. Down to the warm range I was drawn, to sit with my grandfather, for the first time ever. Instantly, I loved him, his white hair and moustache, his dancing eyes and warm hands of welcome, pressing a gift of money into the palm of my hand. I felt him wrap his energy and love around me, as only a grandparent can – it is a love borne out of wisdom, compassion and the innocence of old age and youth. In that short trip, I received a lifetime of love from my grandfather. That trip will be etched in my memory forever. He spent his life, a fisherman on the ocean, and the ocean has a freedom of movement and openness that enables me to breathe, with the greatest of ease. His energy radiated the ocean and I felt embraced and held, in the arms of his ocean. For that, I am deeply grateful. As I write and remember my grandfather, I realise he genetically gifted me his dancing, roguish eyes, the facial feature I love most.

I adored my Father and had him on a pedestal I guess. Strangely he never tumbled off, as most people we put on pedestals do. However, I am conscious of his humanness too. It was how he loved me, that put him there, how he explained things to me so patiently, how he dealt with my fears and anxieties, as I was a very fearful and sensitive child at times. He was ultra patient with me and only once do I remember him losing his temper, when I was unfortunate enough to be caught spitting, for some reason (that must have been a worthy cause!) at the girl, across the road. He called me in and slapped my legs so hard, my Mother begged him to stop. I never did that again and neither did he. He checked for intruders under my bed, lifted out 'daddy-long-legs' and other insects, from the bathroom, went with me into dark rooms upstairs, to check them out before I slept, protected me from big, boisterous dogs and patiently taught me maths and Irish. He also spent endless hours explaining things to me, as knowledge dispels children's fears. I was scared of lots of things, so he had a full time job. It is amusing to watch my patient brother, Father his daughters, in the same way. What a lovely gift my Father made available to his sons. My Father was the parent who was ultra patient with me and my sensitivity. I don't think I would have survived, without this type of nurturing. Of all he gave me, that is what I am most grateful for.

My Mother loved me in a different way. She created a warm, spotlessly clean, comfortable nest, beautiful homemade fresh food and clean clothes, often made by her. She taught me how to knit, sew, embroider, cook, clean, wash my clothes and look after my personal hygiene. She was very strict and disciplined and though this felt like a trap to me, a level of this discipline, stood to me, when times were tough. My sensitivity was very difficult for her, as she did not allow herself, to open up to her own emotions or sensitivity. She was afraid I guess. My Mam had a black leather strap, about a foot long, rounded at each end, and boy did it sting, when you got it on the hands and legs. If she threatened to slap you for misbehaving, she always carried it through, so being scared of her was a good option – it kept us in line. Her father used to slap them with the buckle of his belt, so her strap was much more humane. It is only in the last fifteen to twenty years, that we have found much more humane ways of disciplining our children, without hitting. Society expected you to give your children a beating, to keep them well behaved, up till then. However, the slapping I got did not leave any long term damage. What hurt a lot more was not being able to relate to my Mother, as a sensitive emotional being. My emotions I wore on my sleeve. My Mam's were deeply buried. During my teenage years, I felt a million miles away from her.

I am deeply grateful for the safe haven and cosy nest she provided for me, for her endless hours, of hard work, and love, doing the very best she knew how, for me. Also, the discipline and grounded focus she taught me, has given me a framework that has been vital, when one needs to keep going, no matter what life's challenges are.

Chapter 3

Hormone Heaven

At the tender age of eleven, and having completed fifth class in primary school, which was located a few minutes walk from home, my parents decided to send me, to begin my secondary school education, at an Irish speaking school, which was accessed by travelling on two buses, across Dublin city. Having been schooled through English until then, it was a shock to my system and having to adjust to all subjects being taught through Irish and speaking only Irish during the school day, was in itself a major adjustment, but the straw that broke the camels back, was when my parents decided, that I was so clever at school, that I would bypass sixth class, the preparatory year for secondary school, and jump straight into first year, which was a preparatory year, to adjust to an Irish speaking school, but did not cover or revise the sixth class curriculum.

So I began my secondary education as a young naive innocent eleven year old, feeling like I was thrown into, a 'foreign' speaking school, without the foundation, necessary for the secondary education that was to follow. It felt like a nightmare. The other students were at least a year older; most had been schooled in Irish from the beginning of their education and all had completed sixth class. I felt very nervous all the time, had an almost constant lump in my throat and at times wondered, would I choke and die. It all felt alien to me and I felt abandoned without friends, teachers or a language I was familiar with. The other kids, being older and mostly accompanied by friends from primary school, seemed more confident and street wise, and as regularly happens to timid, quiet, shy children, I was bullied many times, my clothes thrown around, my bag turned upside down and emptied out on the school corridor. I was terrified and began to suffer regularly from irritable bowel, and constantly felt scared and nervous. When I told my parents what was happening, they wanted to visit the head nun, but I went hysterical crying and begged them not to, as I was unbelievably scared, some of the students would make my life a living hell. Many times I felt sorry that my parents did not override my hysteria and visit the head nun. My Mother regretted many times that she did not take me out of this school. She considered it, the biggest mistake she had made with my rearing. However, we never find ourselves where we are not meant to be and there is a golden nugget of wisdom and development to be gathered, in every challenging situation.

My hormones kicked in, with a bang and life changed

from the safe cocoon of childhood, to the roller coaster that often defines, the teenage years. Around this time, my periods began and the pains were so severe, that it necessitated me swallowing up to eight painkillers a day, and often being sent home, looking as white as a ghost. My academics suffered. I suffered on every level. I hated this school, but was to spend seven long years here. Eventually, I found my feet in certain areas – the main one being sport and a great love of sport and movement awoke in me at that time and is still a precious and vital part of my life. My particular passion was basketball and being tall, I was a very good defender and re-bounder (two attributes I sorely needed, to survive, in that secondary school). At every opportunity, early morning, elevenses, lunchtime and evening I played and I felt passionate about it. It was my saviour in so many ways.

Our soul energy sits into our physical body and enables us to function in the Earth, but when we feel threatened or scared, we often reach up towards the heavens, drawing our energy upwards, out of our bodies and it causes us to feel more shaky, weak and powerless. Exercise and physical movement draws our energy down into our bodies, feet and into the Earth, and this enables us to feel more confident, solid and able to cope. Also, exercise and movement, helps to release, built up stress, tension and emotional residues and upheaval, out of the body, through the coccyx or tailbone, the soles of the feet and even the cells and pores breathe and release. We are recharged with new spiritual energy, as we release the old.

So I learned to survive in the school, made some friends and found an outlet for the almost constant stress, fear and tension I was plagued with. The lump in my throat and bowel upset lasted throughout the secondary school process. It was something I lived with. I felt different, very different and the huge sensitivity I had, now that my emotional body was waking up, made it very hard for me to cope at times.

The emotional body or emotional process within you begins to wake up in teenage years and with it comes your fears, insecurities, challenges and eventually an awareness of your gifts and talents in life. So, it's a two sided coin. Your individual uniqueness begins to awaken more fully and also the arenas you have chosen to learn, grow and develop in.

How did I survive? Basketball, singing, domestic science, dancing, all of which I loved, were grounding activities that seemed to earth me and give me confidence. Academic subjects were more challenging though my father was eternally patient and supportive with me. The subjects that had to be learned through Irish were very difficult, like history, which involved learning a lot of facts in a language you were not fluent in, so I memorised it, not understanding very much and ditched the subject, as soon as was possible. Academically I did ok, holding my place in the second of four classes, but I did not shine anything as brightly, as I was capable of. As with every situation in life, when you become familiar with it, no matter how challenging, a certain confidence and ability to cope grows within you. You know the environment and learn to survive within it.

Some of my teachers I loved dearly and when my Irish teacher of the purple hair died, I felt heartbroken. My young physical education and sports teacher I adored and the domestic science nun was so gorgeous, soft, loving and supportive. I became more outgoing, regaling my Mother and sister, with the facts of life, taught through Irish, English and hand actions by a very eccentric nun. The tears rolled down their faces with helpless laughter. It was the most hilarious piece of education I received during secondary school.

I was born with a very heightened awareness or psychic energy, ('psychic' meaning 'of the soul'), an ability of the soul to tune into or pick up, in a very vivid way, peoples thoughts, emotions, attitudes and all that encompasses their lives, and this energy, though awakened in me at birth and early childhood, went asleep to some degree, till teenage years, when it began to reawaken. This makes sense when you consider, a child is cloaked in its mother's auric emanations or electro magnetic field (photographed first by the Russians through Kirlian photography) until about ten or eleven or until the individuality of puberty is born. I was safe, under my mother's cloak till then and I am grateful that I learned what it felt like to be in a safe cocoon. It is important for us to know, it is possible to return to that safe place within us, whenever we need to.

This ability to 'tune in' made my life very difficult. I would walk into a room where students were talking and pick up feelings, thoughts, judgements and criticisms, and it was much later when I realised that I was listening to their thinking and the inner voice of their minds, cells, hearts and souls. This was all mixed up, with the voice of my own inner thoughts and jumbled emotions, so often I felt the criticism was directed at me, but now I am sure, that was not the case at all times. Certain people did have a reaction to my difference and I had a major reaction to it. It took a long time to learn to decipher what was my voice and what were the voices of others. I thought I had a 'screw loose', and never ever spoke to anyone, about what I was feeling and experiencing. Even my Father, who I spoke to about everything in early childhood, I could not speak to about this. It was a closely guarded secret.

Around the age of fifteen or sixteen, I became fascinated by boys and while my first 'real kiss' happened in Co. Clare. I did not have a boyfriend for quite a while after. However, it did not stop me having major crushes on boys and feeling very sexually excited about them. One summer, at the age of sixteen, I went with my friend Ursula and her family, on holiday to a seaside resort in Co. Wexford and I fell in love for the first time, with this gorgeous handsome guy, called Jim. This dark haired, brown eyed Adonis, who I could not take my eyes off or my lips and hands away from, had a broken leg in plaster paris and was on crutches. As we smooched one night, at the edge of a pier, I came close to falling over, but his loving arms and the weight of his plaster cast, rescued me and kept me grounded. Jim was my first love and in the coveted photos, I had a dreamy, faraway, just entered heaven look on my face. It was an innocent love and ended with the holiday. There were many boys after that, none quite measuring up to Jim, all kissy, smoochy, huggable, short lived affairs, but very exciting nonetheless.

I begged my parents, who were very strict, to allow me to discos and Irish dancing ceilis, but while most often the answer was no, I did get to go with my older sister Marian (who acted as my chaperone), at times, much to her disgust, though she managed to turn it, into a very fortuitous event, when the idea of me acting as a decoy, so she could see her new love, awoke in her. So, the needs of all were served. I loved disco dancing and unlike some other girls, who felt shy about dancing, I felt hugely confident when I danced and would dance anywhere, anytime. My spiritual teacher Lilla Bek, told me I had done a lot of sacred dance in past lives. I felt best when I was moving or alone listening to music or reading. Reading was another passion and I read constantly, escaping into the magical world of books.

Someone gifted me a huge poster, divided in sections, with four sets of feet in each section, going through the motions of lovemaking, changing position and colour, from light pink to deep red, as the passion grew. I put it on my bedroom wall, and tried hard to grasp its meaning but when I arrived home from school one day, my Mother said she 'accidentally', knocked it off the wall, and in the process it got torn and she 'had' to burn it. My parents and religious upbringing were very rigid about sexuality and I did not become sexually active, until after my engagement, so scared was I, of God and the Mother.

On a more serious note, I was deeply disturbed one day while coming home on the bus from school, as a girl who was my neighbour and a few years older than me, had a severe epileptic fit. I could feel her choking, thought she was going to die (thankfully she did not), and for many hours, I sat inside my parents bedroom window, looking out at her home, crying. The fear of choking stayed with me for a long time. Given the almost constant lump in my throat, I wondered was that the next thing that would happen. Also, one of my friends younger sisters, died at about fourteen and I will never forget her black curls as she lay so silently in the white coffin, our grief, shock and lack of understanding echoing through the church.

A new happening in my school, one I would have benefited greatly from as a first year, was that as fifth years, we were allocated a first year student, to support and keep a watchful eye on. The lovely gentle blond girl that I 'mothered' was drowned, while attending Irish college in Co. Donegal. A teacher and two students, I was close to died, during my stay at secondary school, and this was to pave the way, for many more experiences of death, early in my life and the learning that ensued, resulted in the healing work I have been able to gift on to others.

At home, during my secondary school years, most especially the early ones, my Mother and I were not having an easy time. Once my emotional self woke up, I was wracked with feelings of not being good enough for my Mother and nothing I did seemed to please her, or at least there was no praise only criticism of me. I felt so upset, trapped and scared at school, so alone, that I was a ball of mixed up emotions, confusion, fear and anger. We had screaming matches. I banged doors, stormed upstairs and answered back. This must have been a nightmare for my Mother, as I had towed the line and tried hard to please up to then, and suddenly she had a screaming, crying monster on her hands. She did not know how to deal with my emotions and neither did I. Things got easier as I advanced through secondary school, but I always felt that she was very hard on me. It was to be much later on that we made our peace.

One other happening, when I was sixteen, changed life in our home forever. My Father was ill and taken into the Mater Hospital in Eccles Street, Dublin, for tests. The hospital was situated just beside my school. I spent every lunch time with him and one day he was very upset, as he told me he had been diagnosed with 'Parkinson's disease'. I tried to soothe and comfort him and asked questions like - Will it kill you? Can it be controlled? Is there medication available so you can live a normal life? In my childlike way, I was trying to see the positive and help him to see it too. Losing my Father was not on my agenda and no way could I go there emotionally. He was my rock and my rock shuddered that day. My Mother was distraught when I got home. It was one of the few times I ever saw her crying. She kept saying – he will never be the same again. In a very subtle way, it was the day the winds changed direction.

It was early sixth year and I was seventeen and preparing for my final exams. A level of career guidance was made available to us, in the form of, a visiting nun from the foreign missions, seeking people for the religious life. Shortly after, we went to visit the 'central remedial clinic', where people who had experienced head and spinal injuries and strokes, went through a programme of rehabilitation. It was during a visit to this clinic, that I had my first real panic attack. A huge fear, like a tidal wave, engulfed me internally, a fear that one of these religious vocations would drop on me and the terror that if they found out I was even thinking about it, I would be forced into following that pathway, despite not wanting it. This fear erupted a thousand times, over the next ten years, dressed in many different guises and only when I was twenty eight did I understand its significance. Again, I never shared it with anyone, but anything could trigger off the utter panic and fear, seeing a nun, being in church, or someone talking about religious vocations. I even became allergic to the word nun. It was my biggest secret and my greatest fear. It would affect me like a standard panic attack, heat rising in my body, pounding heart, sweaty palms, a feeling of utter terror inside and a frantic search to try and understand mentally what was happening to me. At first, I would analyse, debate and investigate it mentally, in its every detail, but so many things would trigger it off, that eventually I just had to breathe through it and let it pass. It was a little like, a mine field; you never knew what you were going to stand on that would cause this internal explosion.

Years later, when I went for healing, I began to understand that we are a sum of many lifetimes experience, wisdom and fears, and that into each lifetime, not only do we take our gathered wisdom, knowledge and love, we also take our unfinished business and new dreams. Yes, into this lifetime, recorded in my every cell, I carried a huge spiritual dream, to learn and grow physically, emotionally and spiritually, but also to gift that learning and the precious wisdom I had gathered in the past, as a healer, teacher and guide to humanity. I discovered that I had spent many lifetimes, in religious life and had felt hugely controlled, restricted and trapped. Despite the joy and fulfilment that was attached to those lifetimes, there was a huge element of sacrifice, (the body was never seen as equal to or worthy of the soul). I was not about to repeat those past experiences.

When I began to focus on career and life after school, I realised that the career guidance experience opened my cells, so I could begin to remember what I came to this World to do and also what I came to heal and learn. Yes, I had and have a huge spiritual vision, but a need to do it, in a way, that nurtures me fully, without sacrifice and heading into a religious order was not the way for me. At that time, I did not understand any of this – all I knew was that I was terrified to share this, in case 'they' (the powers that be) would make me do it. So, I suffered in ignorance and silence for ten years. The fear did lessen as time went by, or my ability to cope with it expanded.

What I really wanted to do, as a career, was to attend 'physical education' college and become a sports teacher in a secondary school. The only college in Ireland was situated in Limerick, which was many hours drive away. My parents told me, they could not afford to send me there, as they were paying for my sister, who was studying to become a froebel teacher, in a college in Dublin. I was gutted, devastated, angry and hurt and it hugely affected my Leaving Certificate results. It did not occur to me at the time, to get a student loan, as I was innocent and most unworldly wise. My parents coaxed me into attending interviews for nursing and primary teaching in Dublin colleges, but no offers came from these interviews, as this was not what I wanted to do, and I even admitted during one interview, that I was there for my parents, not for myself.

Chapter 4

Big Bad Beautiful World

After leaving secondary school, I attended commercial college and being very unhappy there I applied for and got a job, with Coca Cola, as a trainee accountant. I was hugely sensitive and innocent moving out into the World, but somehow the systematic job of working with numbers earthed me and I found, to my amazement, that I was really good, with the game of numbers. Being such a perfectionist, everything was neat, organised and balanced, despite my lack of interest and inability to retain any long term memory of the profit and loss figures. I was never found out! I attended accounting college two nights a week, studying economics, accounting and law. Around the same time, the love of my life "sport" opened a new door to me. I joined a ladies basketball team, working my way up the ranks to play first division and after a period, premier division basketball. It was my passion and it required of me two nights training and one match per week. Between college, basketball, boys, dancing and socialising, there was not a lot of time left for study, so I made the choice not to sit the accounting exams, but continued my training on a practical level and learned quite a lot.

I had become much more outgoing and alcohol and cigarettes gave me the confidence I lacked during social gatherings. However, the next day, I was always very ill, having the shakes, headaches and severe tummy upset. While my friends could continue drinking on a weekend away, my body screamed in outrage and I could not continue. They say that the Stradivarius violin is highly sensitive and plays the most beautiful music, but can easily be knocked off key. My body feels a bit like that. I chose a sensitivity that enables me to attune deeply to the cell memories and patterns of others. To do this, I have to align with divine energies and channel the most sacred love and compassion of the heavens, so I need a most sensitive instrument to do this. My body is easily disturbed by certain foods, like coffee, alcohol, meat and even dairy. I feel better when I eat organic foods or foods next to nature. Of course, I understood nothing about my body's sensitivity, until I was twenty eight and in the meantime, I soldiered on, with my body screaming and roaring, with bronchitis, severe sore throats, irritable bowel and tummy and eventually a possible ulcer. My life did not include emotional expression and as I am first and foremost an emotional feeling being (I always feel first), the pressure to keep that contained in me, was causing physical problems, the precursor to serious illness in a body. We are all emotional beings to one degree or another and the sooner we integrate some emotional education, into our schooling system, the better. The World would be a very different place, as a result.

At the age of twenty one, I met Gerry, my future husband. He was a bright and brilliant young architect. My Mother loved him and talked to him regularly of kitchen extensions and the like. I fell in love with Gerry, in the only way I knew how to fall in love at that time and from the space I was at in my growth and development. We had a lot of fun in the early days, travelling the country, sharing the beauty of the ocean, the mountains, the countryside, beautiful meals and kisses and cuddles. He asked me to marry him very shortly after we met and I said yes and nine months after we met, we were engaged, planning to marry nine months later. I had become very systematic then, putting things in boxes emotionally inside, in order to cope and had an overemphasis on looking perfect and doing everything meticulously. I did not communicate in any depth emotionally with Gerry or anyone else and neither did he communicate emotionally with me. You might wonder how we fell in love and got married. At that time communicating on any deep emotional level was not the norm, so we communicated on the levels we were capable of and familiar with. It was my first most precious dream to marry and have children. When I was younger, I would beg God before I slept, to leave a baby on my bed, during the night, for me to care for. Someone like the baby Jesus would do!!!!!!!!!!!!!

At the ripe old age of twenty two years and seven and a half months, I married Gerry on a crisp cold day; October 20th. 1978. Having a great love of beauty and fashion (the frivolous side of my nature that balances the intense emotional/spiritual journey), I felt like a princess in my wedding dress and after some 'valium' gifted by my Mother, to get me up the isle, I thoroughly enjoyed the day, flitting around like a butterfly, the centre of attention. Our honeymoon took us to Madeira, an island of opposites, opulence and extreme poverty which tore at my heartstrings. It was the first time I had witnessed severe poverty and watching a mother rearing her children under a series of sticks with an old rag pulled over them for shelter, was heart breaking and perhaps it was this sight etched in my mind that has birthed in me, a deep desire, to support, at some time, in some way, healing and balance in what we describe as our third world. It is a basic human right to have food, shelter, clean water, schools, medical care and social structures that support the growth and development of the individual. I find it heartbreaking to see children starving, people without food, water or housing and as there is so much abundance in our Earth, this is scandalous.

My concern and interest is with the cellular memory patterns (something I will explore in detail in a future book), and the resistance we have written in our cells to change, nurturing and abundance for everyone. The macrocosm is a reflection of the microcosm, which means that what we hold as our attitudes internally, reflect in the World around us. We change us and we change the

World. The honeymoon also supplied blue skies, sunlight and beautiful food.

Gerry and I were very different as individuals, he the quiet one, me the more outgoing. We supported each other across that bridge from childhood to adulthood, from leaving home to a home of our own in the big bad World!!! Living with each other before marriage was not an option, as my parents would have disowned me and an insecure sensitive soul like myself, could not have taken that risk at twenty two years of age. I do believe we choose those partners we find ourselves with, before birth. We have a prior agreement with them to grow and develop in a particular way and we have an opportunity to seek balance and freedom, through completing a relationship, we began with them in another lifetime. So Gerry and I were not together by chance – we had a sacred journey to travel together. When we were dating, I chose to leave my job in Coca Cola and work at an accounting job in an architects office, so I would know and understand his business. At that time, I had no awareness of the job I am now doing. Gerry designed a beautiful home, we had built on a half acre site, in the lush green countryside of Co. Meath, some seventeen or eighteen miles from Dublin city.

Nine months or so, after we married and while our home was being built, my Mother became very ill and I became pregnant. My Mam was diagnosed with advanced bowel cancer and had major surgery and the dreaded chemotherapy. I received the news at work and felt emotionally devastated. We had just begun to enjoy a friendship, chats on the phone and I proudly invited her, my Dad and brother Eanna over for dinner. There was so much happening at that time, my Mothers illness, my first pregnancy and our home being built. My Mothers illness came as a huge shock to all of us. Looking back, it was on the cards for a long time, but not having the knowledge then, that I now have, I and we felt powerless to understand it or do anything about it, except to travel that journey with her.

Her operation was major and at some point she was diagnosed with secondary cancer in her liver. Chemotherapy, the most aggressive form of treatment I have ever observed, should not have been given in my opinion, so late in her day. The treatment ravaged her first before the disease took hold. It robbed her of every last shred of energy and even dignity. I watched her being violated by this treatment and I was horrified. It broke my heart and if I could have traded places, at the time, to suffer it for her, I would have. I was just getting to know her and she was being taken away from me. To put it mildly I was devastated. Her first grandchild was on the way and she was never going to see him. I gave up work to be with my Mother, as often as possible.

On one of her better days, before she died, she insisted on being driven out to see our half completed new home. It was a very foggy day and as she was so weak and ill, I wanted to turn back, but she insisted on making the journey. My Mother had a will of iron and the discipline to do anything she set her mind to. So, out she got, aided by two people, onto the uneven terrain of a building site, where she insisted on being supported up a ladder, to take a peep at the upper level. As she came down the ladder, her legs gave way, but she was held on either side, so all was ok. She had a picture of my home now, where I would live with Gerry and where her grandchild would grow up. She came for that picture, to take to the spirit world with her. I still feel the huge emotion of that as I write, some twenty five years later.

During the latter part of my Mothers illness, my aunt Peggy told her, that she had given me a very hard time as I grew up and she asked me about it, but I was not able to discuss it with her at that time.

Before her death, she asked my Father to buy her a warm red fur dressing gown. He complied, and did not question her even though she had many dressing gowns and did not need another one. He left it at the end of her bed and one day she said to me, you can wear that when you are having the baby. It was her last gift to me, so I would have part of her wrapped around me at that time.

Mam never spoke of her death, how she felt or how we felt. In the tradition of our conditioning, we tried not to cry in front of her. She came home for a few days the Christmas before she died, eating little and asking us not to put up the Christmas tree. She had created such magical Christmases for us, a gift I handed onto my children, that this Christmas must have been utterly heartbreaking for her. As she left the house for the last time to return to hospital, she visited each room for a few moments, gathering her memories to take with her. The voice and feeling of what she was doing echoed through the walls and filled the house. It felt earth shattering.

The few days before Mam died, I sat a lot with her and she reached up many times, opening and closing the buttons of my beautiful 'Laura Ashley' maternity dresses. She would talk about the baby but I could not understand what she was saying. The morning of her death she was unable to speak and as I was in the room alone with her, her eyes followed me everywhere. I regret not holding her hand – there was no touch in our home, you got a hug if you got engaged or married but that was it. I regret not having learnt how to cross those barriers, wrap my arms around my Mam and hold her as she was dying. My love was holding her for sure, but I really regret the touch part. Many years later, I went on a meditative healing journey, to her deathbed and held and kissed her. When something remains undone, we can at any stage venture into the past through a meditative journey, and do what we need to do.

My Mother died that day, at forty seven years of age, on 8th February 1980, as gently as a breeze shimmering across a lake. We were all there, my Dad, her sisters and her children, and of course in my tummy, her first grandchild. After she died, I watched her face change to that of a sixteen year old beauty, with dark hair. Perhaps that is the age she wanted to revisit, the age she felt most free. Through her funeral, I cried oceans of tears and many people were very worried about me and the baby. I could not understand my young Mother, being in this coffin, going into the Earth. My Father was heartbroken – his beautiful bride was gone. I always bought my Mam orchids as she really loved them, so I put one in her hand before the coffin closed – my last gift to her.

Later, I understood my Mothers illness, death and rebirth into the spiritual realm, which is after all our real home. We are only visitors to this planet. As individuals we bring many things to the Earth, our uniqueness and individuality (after all there is only one of each of us), our love, our wisdom, gifts and talents, our dreams and unfinished business or challenges. My Mam's journey was about many wonderful things, being born, growing up, falling in love, giving birth to and rearing us, developing her exquisite needlework, fashion design and homemaking skills, and so forth.

The challenge that led to her death/rebirth was about emotions and sensitivity. She experienced extreme constipation and regularly took medication to try and regulate her bowel. The bowel governs release of food and emotional waste from the body. If we hold on tightly in our cells, a little like clenching our fists, when we are afraid, it creates an energy blockage in the body and over long periods, if there is no release or letting go mechanism, happening in the body, it can create serious illness in the organs. Energy needs to flow. It is a little like water – if you contain it the pressure builds up and up and eventually something has to give to release the pressure. There is a powerful spirit energy source flowing through our bodies. We are in effect pure energy and for optimum health, we need to be engaging in activities and expression that support the free flow of this energy through us into the Earth. We need a balance of activity and rest, exercise, healthy diet but most importantly we need to communicate and express ourselves, our feelings, dreams, needs and so on. We need to be seeking to nurture ourselves fully and completely and then share ourselves with others in whatever ways are comfortable. We most often live the other way around, meeting the needs of others and the outside world before we even consider our own needs.

My Mother was a lot like this. She considered the neighbours a lot and presenting to the outside world what she thought was needed for acceptance and love I guess. Apart from keeping her hair, nails and clothes meticulously, my memory is that she worked tirelessly. I don't remember her ever taking much time to nurture herself as an individual. I wonder even when she tweezed her eyebrows and filed her nails, was it a duty for the outside world or did it give her any pleasure? I hope it did. She held everything emotionally, creating a continued tightness in her tummy and bowel area. If I ever came to her with an emotional issue (me being a ball of water), her reply was to forget about it and get on with it – no over indulgence allowed. She did not indulge herself at all, until perhaps she got sick and though she did not speak about her illness, I noticed something new and gentle about her. Constipation and duty are two words I associate with my Mother, and I sense, that she had a deep emotional sensitivity that was disciplined out of all proportion and buried under a lot of fear. Perhaps we are more alike than I ever thought possible and I am blessed to be living in an era, where there are outlets and possibilities to develop ones emotional self. I hardly ever saw her cry or express a feeling, unless she was angry with us or my Dad.

Her bowel cancer came from a lifetime of holding on tightly to her emotions and perhaps hidden dreams and having no outlet for expression or release. We all hold on and become tight and stressed at times, when we are afraid, very busy, in difficult situations, have a lot of responsibility or attitudes and expectations of ourselves that are unreasonable, but once there is a release every now and then or a stepping towards a solution, a letting go in someway, our energy heals and rebalances itself. A holding on has to be set in stone within us to cause a serious illness, as the body energy naturally seeks health, balance and harmony at all times.

The tiniest changes can make a dramatic difference to our bodies and lives. I understand the liver cancer my Mam experienced when I look at how the liver filters the blood stream, processing toxic waste both physical and emotional. It is an amazing organ, capable of recharging and renewing itself so efficiently, so it is an extreme, can not go any further situation, when the liver develops a malignant tumour. Every part of my Mother's body, mind, emotions, energy and soul had to be screaming for release, let go and rebirth, and watching her face change after she died, let me know loud and clearly, that she was flowing free again. Her wings were outstretched and she was soaring and happy I feel. She made her change, through her illness, death and rebirth into spirit. It was her journey, her way and it must have been the only way her body and soul saw possible to make this transformation.

It is my dream to share with the Earth, what I have learnt about processing our emotions and soul journey, in order to keep our bodies healthy and functioning well in the Earth, until we are ready to go. Of course my Mam would have loved to hold her first grandchild and all her grandchildren and enjoy growing into mature wise old age, experiencing all the pleasures that time in our lives has to offer. But the soul and spirit has to fly free, no matter what.

I was twenty three and enormously pregnant when my Mother died. Often, as one soul is gifted to a family, another soul leaves or rather that is my personal experience. My pregnancy was over shadowed by my Mam's death, but I was silently very excited about the new babe growing inside me and loved being pregnant. Around the time of my Mam's death, I experienced protein in my urine and fluid retention, which are two indicators of possible toxaemia. My Mother also had symptoms of toxaemia during pregnancy. About three weeks after her death, at almost thirty five weeks pregnant, I had a show and was hospitalised for early delivery. After many invasive rectal internals, I was placed in a ward with five other women, to await the true onset of labour.

Opposite me there was a girl of seventeen or eighteen and she said, 'do you mind if I ask you something?' 'What is it like to have sex or make love'? Considering she was sitting there awaiting the birth of her baby, her question seemed unbelievable. She went on to explain that she was from a wealthy family and while away at boarding school, she fell in love with a local lad and he being below her station (from her parents viewpoint), she was forbidden to see him. However, during a dance to celebrate leaving school, a lovers exchange with her chosen one, saw him release those sperm beings, close to an area that was fertile and waiting. There was no penetration and no sex as such, but the hand of fate stepped in and she became pregnant. Her parents disowned her but her loyal lad, stepped in, took care of her and found a place for them to live. They never made love as they were too fearful of hurting the baby. The poor angel had to have her hymen ruptured under anaesthetic, before her baby was born. The last time I saw this innocent young girl, she was been wheeled down to delivery. I inquired and the nurse said her baby was born well and healthy.

Most of the women in the ward had given birth. I rambled in and out of labour, scolded by one of the nurses for stopping my labour. The truth was the women screaming and moaning in the corridors did not instil much confidence in me and I was scared of the unknown and learning fast that this hospital had a silent catholic policy of no pain medication, unless you were near death and they had to revive you!!! Torture was the order of the day. I thanked God later for my Mother's discipline and my ability to visualise from past life experience (certainly no conscious experience up to that point in this lifetime).

The second night in the ward was very stressful. A mother, who had just given birth to an eight pound stillborn baby girl, was placed in our ward, with me, an expectant mother and other mother and new baby pods. I was outraged at the insensitivity of those that placed her in this ward. The only mark of respect was that all of our curtains remained drawn. She cried through the night in her tent and I cried through the night in mine. She cried for her baby, the life together they would never share. I cried for my Mam and for that young bereaved mother and for the deep sadness of it all. I ached to go and sit with her and hold her hand, but I was young and unconfident and had not got the courage to do so. The next day she went home. I hope her heart has healed.

Back in my own ranch, the contractions were kicking in with a bang. Labour had taken three or four days to become fully established and epidurals and all pain relief I had requested and been promised was denied me, on the false grounds that the baby was premature. Labour was intensely painful, most especially in my lower back and clutching a leaflet I was given about how to breathe and visualise during contractions, I set about focusing on and completing the job at hand, with the self same discipline my Mother had gifted me. If she could do it, so could I. Each wave took 100% of my focus and attention. I became the waves breaking on the shore. The desire to strangle my Mother kicked in, between waves, as I remembered her telling me that contractions were like strong period pains – definitely not true. There was a moment when I wanted to leave the Hospital and not give birth at all, impossible as that was.

With great gusto, (the midwives trying to slow me down), I pushed my tiny first born baby son, into the earth on the eight of March 1980, exactly a calendar month after my Mother had died. He weighed in at four pounds fourteen ounces and had spent thirty five and a half weeks in the womb. We almost shared a birthday. I fell instantly, head over heels in love with him. He was still covered in angel dust, the imprint of his heavenly wings being almost visible.

I felt elated and proud of myself for the first time ever and felt I had just completed the most wonderful job in the world. Birth opens the spiritual corridors that link us to heaven and just as I received a divine beautiful child, I also got a dose of self worth and confidence and the most powerful surge of love I had ever experienced.

I held my beautiful baby, then Gerry arrived to share in the magic, but it was not long before they insisted on taking him to an incubator in intensive care, as he was so premature. A day or so later, he was in trouble, yellow, jaundiced and proving very difficult to wake up or breastfeed. His Bilirubin levels were not good and a nurse came and told me he needed an instant blood transfusion and in the same breath she suggested they do an emergency baptism. Gerry was visiting one of his projects on a building site and could not be contacted.

They took the three quarters of a pint of blood the baby needed, for his entire body from me and a short time later I was called for his baptism. I was all alone and very scared. Having just lost my Mam, I did not want to lose my baby, so I implored, begged, pleaded with heaven not to take him from me. I chose his name 'Kenn' (the translation of the Irish name Cian), going up the stairs. My hands shook so badly, I could not hold him during the emergency baptism, so I asked the nurse to do me the honour, in case I dropped him. He was tiny, blissfully asleep during the process of his baptism and tube feeding.

A sleepless night followed, but thankfully he stabilised and they called him the little vampire who flourished on his mother's blood. The staff had expected to transfuse him many times, to stabilise him. Heaven was smiling on us.

I would wrap myself up in my soft red dressing gown (courtesy of my Mother) many times a day, and with my very sore, stitched and bruised ass, waddle my way to intensive care, on the top floor of the hospital, to breastfeed tiny baby Kenn. On one of these visits, the doctor in charge asked to see me, accused me of not giving the baby glucose, told me he was not doing well on my breast milk and I was no longer allowed to feed him, as he had lost a lot of weight. I was emotional, devastated, judged and demeaned as a new mother, and I felt the baby was feeding very well and had lost no weight, though it can be normal to lose a little after birth. There was no softness or support for me whatsoever, so I decided to leave the hospital, angry and upset and go home. I would express breast milk for them to feed him by bottle and visit the hospital twice a day to feed him myself. Considering I lived in Co. Meath, some eighteen miles from this hospital, my new routine was some feat. Every day I visited, with sterilised containers of expressed breast milk and when the time came to take baby Kenn home, whose mouth and throat were now covered in thrush (from the bottles I felt at the time) and painted with purple 'gentian violet', a nurse took me aside, explaining that there was a discrepancy between the scales in the labour ward and the scales in the intensive care unit. In the labour ward, the baby weighed in at five pounds three and a half ounces and in intensive care, a half hour after birth, he weighed in at four pounds fourteen ounces, some five and a half ounces lighter, which is a considerable difference for a small baby.

He had in fact lost no weight as I had thought and the nurse said they were releasing him early, as he was doing much better with his mother than in the hospital. There was no apology from the abusive insensitive doctor, but I am grateful to the nurse for her honesty, as it helped restore my confidence. At the time I was unable to express myself or communicate my feelings, so I bottled it all up inside, but I felt very upset about the way I had been treated in this supposedly, time honoured, well established Dublin maternity hospital.

Bringing my baby home was both beautiful and painful. He spent a number of weeks in an incubator, after I discharged myself. Gerry and I went to collect him and as I was all 'fingers and thumbs', Gerry dressed him in his tiny premature vest, babygro and white wrap around cardigan, that had taken me seven months to knit! Kenn's first stop in the outside world was at my parent's home. This baby was the little ray of sunshine that helped soothe my Father's heart. I wanted and needed to put baby Kenn into my Father's arms first. I ached to put him into my Mother's arms and missed her so badly at that time. I was the first one to give birth in my family and I did not have any other babies or children in my immediate environment, so I cared for and reared Kenn on pure intuition and love and if I had a problem I asked my Dad. Luckily I was a natural Mother and took to the task, like a duck to water. Living in Co. Meath felt isolating and lonely in the beginning. My little ray of sunshine kept me busy and though mothering came naturally, grieving for my Mother did not and so I did the only thing I knew how to do, by zipping up my grief in a secure box within me.

The symptoms of Parkinson's, the disease my Father suffered from, were becoming more severe, so he retired from his position as principal of a large boys primary school and before long, he could no longer drive. It must have been heartbreaking for him, as teaching was his vocation. He missed my Mother enormously. There was no emotional or grief language in our house, so we just got on with it, as best we could. Baby Kenn and I spent as much time, as we could manage with my Dad. Gerry's Mam was very loving and supportive, a nicer mother-in-law one could not have wished for, but living an hour's drive away, we did not get to see each other very often.

I became a stay at home Mum, as my heart yearned to be with my baby. There was virtually no support with Kenn in those early days, so feeding him every two to three hours for six months, with matchsticks positioned to keep my eyes open, was my new life. I was deeply in love with my new baby. He was kissed, cuddled, gobbled up and sang to, even when he regurgitated most of his milk on top of me and had to be fed time and time again. There were exhausted stars in my eyes but my heart sang with the delight of it all.

Meanwhile, in a very subtle way Gerry and I were drifting apart. Emotionally, I was struggling, but perhaps ignoring the struggle. I would only get away with that for a few more years, before emotional collapse and spiritual emergence and rebirth, became the only way to go.

Chapter 5

Family Expansion

When Kenn was a year and six months old, Gerry and I took him to Rhodes, Greece, for his first foreign holiday. The day before we left, I discovered to my delight, that I was pregnant, so the early weeks of my growing babe's life were spent in the very hot August sunshine of Rhodes. Greek salads and a particular type of cream cake, became the only foods my turbulent tummy would accept, but when I brought the self same 'feta' carefully packaged in brine, home with me, my tummy would somersault every time I opened the fridge, so it had to leave with the bin man.

Perhaps, twelve or fourteen weeks into the pregnancy, I had a bleed and was taken to hospital (a much more humane one), where I was sedated for about five days, in the hope that I would not lose the baby. It was discovered I had 'placenta previa', which is a low lying placenta that can be prone to haemorrhaging. The pregnancy stabilised, but I had signs of blood on a number of occasions and had to be confined to bed or hospitalised, so I opted for a locked bedroom and a box of toys, so I could rest and Kenn could play. With this type of pregnancy condition, the danger of haemorrhaging was one I lived with. As I lived out in the country with a one year old and no car at that time, I fantasised about stopping the first car that passed my home, if I needed a quick entry to hospital.

In early January of 1982, when I was almost seven months pregnant, the worst snow conditions I ever remember in Ireland, hit the country. I had gone to visit my Dad and as conditions were deteriorating, I decided it was time to leave for home, some thirty minutes drive away, not realising how dangerous driving conditions were. I drove through the Phoenix Park, a vast nature reserve and parkland in the Dublin area and my car got stuck in a snowdrift. With my big pregnancy bump and leaving Kenn strapped into his baby seat, I slid and waddled to the main road and was close to kneeling and begging someone to stop and help, as the drivers were scared of stopping their cars, in case they too got stuck, when eventually, help came in the guise of a male angel, who got me moving again. I collected Gerry from his office and we attempted to drive home. There were blizzard conditions and with one lane open and walls of snow rising up either side of the car, it was a little like driving in a snow tunnel. We were forced to turn back and seek shelter. Luckily some friends took us in and we remained snowed in for the best part of a week. The men tracked seven miles across the fields to get supplies from our freezer, when the food ran low. The driveway to our home had a solid packed snowdrift, some seven foot high. We all had cabin fever when the thaw finally hit.

About two weeks later, I developed very high blood pressure and was hospitalised for a month, before the baby was born. Though my sister Marian lovingly looked after Kenn, he would at times curl up and howl for me. He must have felt abandoned or that I was never coming back as I was the constant in his life.

My previous maternity hospital experience had been a difficult one, and this time I was more aware of asking for my needs, such as; no rectal examinations, no enemas and an epidural and pain medication available if I needed it. I had a consultation with this gem of an obstetrician, Hubert O'Connor, presenting my needs and his reply was 'anything you want my dear'. My medical insurance covered me to give birth in a private hospital and this medical experience turned out to be a vastly different one to the first. This 'divine doc' came to see me seven days a week, during my six week stay in hospital and he cared for me so expertly, meeting my needs in everyway possible. Medication, bed rest and a foetal heart monitor were the order of the day, as the baby's movements were minimal.

My fear during this pregnancy was that I would not be able to love a second baby, as much as I loved Kenn, but now the winds of fear had altered direction and my life and the baby's were what I feared losing

I was experiencing horrendous abdominal pain at times

and at thirty eight weeks the doctor decided to give me a caesarean section, as medication and very high blood pressure were adversely affecting me and the baby. The night before the section I was terrified but the calming influence of my Dad, Gerry and my sister Marian were beside me. Having a catheter in was a horrible and unpleasant experience and a delay of a number of hours in theatre, left me vulnerable and anxious about the unknown element of surgery and its effects. However, when I arrived in theatre to be confronted by the 'divine doc' clad in white wellies and gown, I was overcome by a need to tease him about his attire, which I guess relaxed me a little. My last memory was saying the word ether, as I could taste it vividly in my mouth the second I was injected. My next memory was Gerry waking me, to tell me we had a baby son, but I was so drugged that my span of attention was a number of seconds and I don't think I processed anything about the baby at that time.

I became vaguely conscious, in terrible pain, clutching a bell which I rang regularly, begging for morphine. The staff said I would be unconscious if they administered anymore – it was a good option from where I was feeling! When I became more conscious and aware of my surroundings that evening, I asked for my baby and he was placed in my arms, a black haired baby boy of almost eight pounds, who we named Davin. In my drugged state, I wondered was he mine as he looked so different to Kenn and I had not been conscious at his birth (this is a common initial feeling with mothers whose babies are born under anaesthetic). However, I cuddled him, fed him and fell instantly head over heels, in love with my beautiful new baby boy and knew beyond shadow of a doubt, that he was mine. We curled up together and fell asleep. He smelled divine, of heaven and my mother (he must have carried in her scent to soothe and support me) and he became part of my skin, with the greatest of ease.

My fears of not loving him, as much as Kenn were unfounded. I realised very quickly, that we have an unlimited and vast reservoir of love in our hearts. In those early days, I fed baby Davin lying down, as I was unable to sit up, never winding him (he just did not seem to have any wind) and regularly I was scolded for falling asleep in the bed with him. He was a very quiet easy newborn and caring for him, took minimal energy in those early days. Being two weeks premature, he spent a few days in an incubator.

The first few days I was in and out of consciousness, very heavily medicated and in a lot of pain. As things eased and I began to move around, the 'divine doc' told me I was a very lucky girl. I said – because the baby lived? He said – because you did. I asked no questions or details, but a little research years later, confirmed that I haemorrhaged, just as my mother had when I was born. The horrendous pain before birth was an internal bleed and so the level of pain I experienced after the birth, was in no way indicative of the average C Section. I had experienced my third near death experience and I attributed my life, to the care and expertise of this divine talented doctor and his team, and my desire to stay alive of course. He warned me many times, that if I were to become pregnant during the following year, it would most likely kill me. He jokingly told me to lock Gerry in the bathroom.

About seven days after my C Section, my brother Barry was marrying his Tracy and I asked for permission to attend the reception for a few hours. Many of the medical staff, even ones I had not had the pleasure of meeting, came to visit me, in awe of the one, who had almost died and was determined to go to the wedding. Permission was given, for a short time and I dissolved into tears when I saw Tracy, who felt like a sister, looking exquisitely beautiful on her big day. I was so very weak and just about survived the meal and one brandy, before returning to give my baby son, his first alcohol flavoured milk. We both slept for twelve hours.

The cocoon of the hospital and the mindful and loving care of the 'divine doc' and staff held me, in those early days. However, when I went home there was no one to hold me. I had almost died, was standing like an L bend, most often against the wall, weak as water, having had major surgery and was responsible for the care of a new baby and a two year old. It was without a doubt the most physically demanding year of my life. The local health nurse was my lifeline, calling to see me about twice a week and keeping a watchful eye over me. Gerry worked five to six days a week and sometimes at night also, so I struggled on very alone, without any support. I would lie against the sand coloured brick wall in the kitchen, every now and then, when I felt exhausted, and it was quite a while before I could stand up straight. I felt a million miles away from Gerry at this time. We were not connecting, communicating or supporting each other. We had both stepped into traditional roles I guess. Gerry became the breadwinner as his father had before him and I became the one that reared the children and ran the house, just as my Mother had.

Our cells record the imprint of the first adult relationship that we have encountered. It becomes our blueprint or springboard to where we want to go. Our first instinct is to copy those patterns that we have observed, even if our needs are very different to those of our parents and we are screaming inside for something different. I was silently screaming inside for something different and emotionally I was heading towards overload. It is fair to say as we get older, we review the patterns that we copy from those around us, and it gives us an opportunity to delete what is not applicable to us as individuals, so we can live life on our own terms.

Every ounce of my energy at this time went into surviving the physical demands of every day. I loved being a mother, it was natural and easy for me on so many levels, but the physical demand of trying to recover, run a home and care for two babies was hugely challenging. I had no emotional outlet and no physical support and still the nun phobia would rear its head every now and then.

During this time I had a terrifying dream, that a giant spaceship of the most brilliant white light I had ever seen, landed outside my bedroom window and I saw many light people coming to get me. I was running and hiding, terrified they would catch me and knowing somewhere inside they eventually would. I woke shaking and scared and saw a flash of that brilliant light as I awoke. Later, I understood that dream to be the entry into the spiritual and emotional world of my sacred journey and all the work I had to do to get there. And boy was I scared of it. The word scared and sacred seem to be very connected, perhaps because we are most scared of our own power, that which is most sacred within us, we feel unworthy of. My journey, all of our journeys are about falling in love with ourselves, knowing our worthiness, embracing the power of who we are, and sharing our gifts and who we are with the World around us. We are all gifted in our own unique and individual way. Let us not forget that we are never better than or above another, nor are we worse than or lower than another. We are equal, yet individual and different, like a precious masterpiece gifted to the World. That is why a newborn baby is unique, heaven kissed and divine and we are unique, heaven kissed and divine throughout every aspect of our lives, even when we are behaving in a very hurt, unloving and aggressive manner.

Giving birth, opens the spiritual centres, aligns a person with their chosen role in life, thus opening the emotional body, giving us an opportunity to process what is necessary, in order to express our dreams and gifting us what we need from the heavens to support us on our way. All, that is gifted to us, and awoken in us, through the opening of the birth corridors, awaits collection, when we are ready or have time to claim and process all that we are. The soul comes and leaves the body through the top of the head and that is why the fontanel at the top of the head is open at birth and again at the moment of death.

Haemorrhaging; the spilling of blood is about sacrifice traditionally and in many past lifetimes I have sacrificed myself for spiritual gain. This has been done by the masses through many lifetimes. Religions teach that our body is unworthy of our soul. Our prayers are filled with reference to weakness of the flesh. So, we have recorded in our cell memories, the imprint of that sacrifice and pain, just as the body records a scar and repeats it again and again, even though the cells renew themselves.

Across the world in this lifetime, we are seeking to work with the process of healing those sacrifice patterns and knowing that our bodies, are sacred and worthy of, and equal to our soul. At best, we can set in stone a blueprint whereby the World at large can heal those sacrificial body imprints, in the future in whatever time frame is necessary. Clearing memory patterns is akin, to the ocean wiping footprints from the sand.

I carried in sacrifice patterns to heal, and that is why I tried to leave so many times this lifetime, because I chose to do so much spiritual work within myself and the Earth, and I have never before done it without sacrifice, and the pain of sacrificing myself again, is a fate, worse than death. This lifetime I am choosing to learn to live and work without sacrifice. So, my birth and my baby's birth make a lot of sense to me. The spilling of that blood opened a door in my body that would enable me, little by little, to release old sacrifice patterns, clearing the way and aligning me with what I came to do. There is nothing that happens in our lives that does not offer us an opportunity to learn, grow and gather a sacred precious jewel of awareness and wisdom, along the way.

Chapter 6

The Awakening

Around this time, a family happening that I am not at liberty to discuss here, saw me spending the vast majority of a two week period, in a hospital. It was an exhausting time and in the middle of it all, I had a miscarriage. Having missed a period, but not realising I was pregnant, one fateful day I passed something large, that I knew to be a miscarriage. Some time later in the hospital canteen I had a horrible intense panic attack, which was very scary. I had not planned on having another baby, as I was concerned about my health, so on a logical rational level the miscarriage was not an issue, but on an emotional body/hormone level, I was in upheaval and also exhausted and worn out. I was on a downward spiral of emotional overload and about to collapse. During the previous few years, I had suffered various health issues from sore throats and severe bronchitis to a severe kidney infection, through which I was bleeding from my kidneys at the onset and medicated for five months, alongside a possible tummy ulcer that was treated with the strong drug 'tagamet'. All in all my body was manifesting symptoms of distress and depletion on all levels.

My sister Marian and friend Ursula, very kindly took the children, while Gerry and I went to the Canary Islands, for a much needed holiday. While there, I experienced severe food poisoning, lost a lot of weight, could not sleep, had regular panic attacks and was in total disarray emotionally and physically. I managed to hide the reality of my situation, until I returned home and found it close to impossible to cope with normal life. Driving the car or going to the supermarket became a nightmare as I had constant panic attacks, my heart was pounding, I could not breathe, I could not cope with my thoughts or anything else, I thought I was going crazy or going to die and so very terrified 'they' would lock me up. All I had hidden and locked away for so long was tumbling out and the wall behind which I hid was tumbling down. I was terrified of drugs, mental hospitals, and electric shock treatment and so scared I had schizophrenia. I had never once spoken about my internal world to anyone, lest I be locked up and the key thrown away. I was really scared of what was going on inside me, but even more scared of how I would be treated in the World outside me.

I was twenty seven years and six months old when this crisis happened and astrologically this is the time in your life when the planet Saturn, called 'the teacher', returns to the place it held at the time of your birth. This planet moves through the constellation of your birth sign for two and a half years and it was this next two and a half years that changed my life forever. So, the areas you need to pay attention to and work with, are presented to you during this time, in order to enhance your life and breathe fire into your dreams.

A trusted friend told me to snap out of it. There was no one around me who could support me with this. Even my Dad said – "don't tell me you are getting like your grandmother", who had a nervous breakdown at some stage. She was a sensitive and the kindred spirit who held me after my birth. I was desperately scared, unable to sleep, losing a lot of weight, having horrendous panic attacks, but strangely enough, none of this effected me rearing the children. My two beautiful little boys kept me earthed and my feet on the ground, I am so grateful to them for needing me at that time, because if they were not there, I might not have chosen to stay on the planet. They were without a doubt my reason for living.

Not knowing where to turn, I sent for the doctor, who presented me with my worse fears, telling me I would get a lot worse, lock myself in the bedroom and be taken to hospital, if I did not take the medication he was prescribing, which he said was very mild. He lied and he bullied me. The drugs were so strong, that I felt locked in a bubble I could not get out of. There was a feeling that I was drifting up to the ceiling, so I promptly threw the drugs in the bin. I could not be removed from my children in that way. I needed to be fully alert to their needs, not a zombie. My emotional pain was better, more real that that.

One day while visiting my Dad, a chance meeting and chat at a local shop with Nancy, the mother of one of my closest friends, (who I felt I could tell a little to) resulted in her suggestion that I make an appointment with Tony Hogan, a spiritual healer. This turned out to be a major turning point in my life. I felt desperate and though I consciously knew nothing about spiritual healing, I made an appointment to see Tony.

A door opened the day of my first appointment, I will be forever grateful for. This window of opportunity, I jumped through with every ounce of my being, like a fish to water. I was starving for spiritual and emotional sustenance. My first appointment with Tony was one of huge release. As I sat in front of him and cried and cried, feelings I had never shared with anyone came tumbling out. I told him in detail about the 'nun fear' I experienced and he nodded and smiled. He seemed to understand everything I said and was so very calm and gentle with me. He then put me lying on a plinth, told me to close my eyes and he put his hands on my head and tummy. I felt a sensation, like a wave of energy, running up and down my spine and I fell into a deeply relaxed state.

After the appointment, I felt calmer, a little easier for perhaps a few hours or a day, but worried about what I had experienced. What was in his hands? What was running up and down my body? What was he doing? Could he harm me? I was in a complete state of emotional overload, exhaustion and collapse and highly sensitive like a live wire, so everything scared me and I trusted nothing or no-one, but I had a glimmer of hope now. My brother-in-law drove me to appointments with Tony, twice a week, for a time, until I felt able to drive myself. My first question to Tony's secretary, on my second visit, was did I have schizophrenia? She laughed and said "no you don't." I was relieved and that particular fear dispersed into thin air.

The early days of visiting Tony, felt like being put on an oxygen mask for a while and that energy he channelled, created an ease within me, which lasted for short periods at first that gradually extended over time to give me much greater ease. He gave me a simple meditation to practice, that began with imagining light slowly entering my toes and feet, then step by step taking it through my body, until I visualised myself a glowing radiant being of light. Teaching me to meditate and encouraging me to practice every day, was the greatest gift Tony gave me. It was the continuous practice of this exercise that broke the long six traumatic months of sleepless nights. After a time, I would arrive at my knees and be fast asleep. If everything I owned was taken from me, the one thing I could not live without is meditation and it is the one thing that can never be taken from you. All answers come from within and if we go within, the burden instantly begins to ease.

Later, I understood that there is a 'universal' or 'spiritual' energy, we all feed from and are created from. We all radiate this energy or life force and every living thing has an aura or force field of energy surrounding it. Technically we all gift each other energy all the time as we interact, but very sensitive people with a healing ideal, learn how to act as a conduit or channel to gift a wave of universal energy, to help re-energise a person when they are emotionally or physically in need and this supports the person to realign, with their own centre and spirit energy source.

For a number of months before I went to Tony, I felt as if I was hanging onto the edge of a cliff by my fingernails and though this feeling continued for quite some time, I now saw the light clearly at the end of the tunnel. Therein lay the answers to my questions and little by little I would claim them. In the beginning with Tony I was learning survival techniques and receiving powerful energy boosts to keep me here, as I felt so abandoned, alone, isolated and different to all those around me. Mixed up inside me were my own jumble of emotions and all that I tuned into with other peoples emotional patterns and soul journeys. I was a ball of pain and confusion.

Though I have learnt over twenty years to know myself, there are still moments when I tune into situations and am confused as to whether they are mine or someone else's. Like yesterday, I was driving to have lunch with a friend, to celebrate her birthday and as the traffic was heavy, I reached for the phone to call her and a wave of nausea washed over me and suddenly out of the blue I felt really ill. It had abated a little when I arrived at the restaurant, but it only disappeared completely, as I spoke to my friend and realised she had been feeling really ill and was dealing with emotional upheaval. As she spoke and cried, I felt well again. This has happened to me a thousand times.

It is the deciphering of the energies that is the challenge. It also feels like someone asks me for healing on a silent mental wavelength and I sometimes feel a sensation as a way of receiving that message and when I channel the healing requested, balance is restored inside me.

Tony taught me about diet and I began to eat a lot of fruit, vegetables, salads and whole grains and also take supplements like B complex and Brewers years for stress, and calcium to feed the nerve endings and help restore my sleep pattern. In time I gave up alcohol and smoking as I was pretty much allergic or super sensitive to everything I put in my mouth at that stage, so back to basics and natural eating was the only way to go. In the early days with Tony I was having two healing sessions a week and often I would have horrendous panic attacks and feel totally unable to cope. At these times, I knew I could call Tony's secretary, who also had beautiful healing energy, for a few moments reassurance or a reminder to keep breathing. They were the only people I could talk to and have moments of support from at that time. There was no-one in my everyday life who understood any of this, so there was nowhere to go, but inside me to meditate, time and time again. It was a long hard climb up my Mount Everest, but I am proud I stuck with the journey, as it made me who I am today.

The biggest fear I lived with during that time and for quite some time after, was that I was going to go mad, lose my mind and be locked up in a mental hospital. Having Mercury, the planet of the mind, in the air sign of Aquarius (astrologically), meant that I had a lot of mind activity and capabilities, but in those early days it manifested as a mind that was racing day and night and felt completely deranged and out of control. From the age of eleven, my mind raced, trying to control and understand things, but by the time I went to Tony, it moved like raging rapids and I felt terrified of it. I suffered the most intense pain up the back of my neck and around the top of my head like a claw. It was my mind, not my emotions I was most frightened of, as I could not shut it up, quieten it down or appease it in anyway. Many times I thought if I could only take my head off and give it away, all would be okay. I learned little by little, that my mind was trying to control my emotions, keep them at bay and under wraps, in case God forbid, they spilt out into the World around me. This was not the done thing in my World. Only people that were mentally ill and emotionally unstable did this. But I had reached the end of the road doing this, as the container of my body was full and just like a boiling kettle needs a vent to release its steam, I needed to express my feelings and empty out what was inside.

Tony suggested I write and though I was resistant to the idea for a while, once I started, I could not stop and it made a dramatic difference to me and my life. The saying 'if you want to know me come and live with me', applies first to oneself. In order to have a loving, compassionate and healthy relationship with ourselves, we need to spend time with ourselves and listen to ourselves. Writing is a safe and effective way to express feelings wholeheartedly, without having to please another or watch ones 'p's and q's', in case of being judged or unloved. It is strange at this point in the book, I am feeling I should put in some nice bits, in case people feel the book is too intense or depressing and then I realise that writing this book signifies the end of a pattern of trying to please, that I have been working with all my life. As I started life feeling guilty and desperately wanting to please, so I would be good enough to be loved, I realise that I have always tried to package and present myself in a way that would please people. Just as the private writing in my diary gave me permission to have a private voice and get to know myself, this book is giving me permission to express my voice fully and clearly in this World and nothing can be packaged or presented to please, but honestly and compassionately shared as the true voice of my story, or the main events of it at any rate. As Oprah says, if a story supports even one person, it is worth telling. It has taken me a long time to arrive at this point, but giving myself permission to express my voice fully in the Earth, is my greatest gift to myself and sharing it with you is the icing on the cake.

As I wrote in my diary, I cried an ocean of tears and though I felt raw, scared and emotional, I was emptying out, letting go, making sense of me and my life. I experienced the feeling of huge weights being released from within me. I had a format in place now, where I could journey through this breakdown or breakthrough. This journey took me further away from rather than closer to Gerry and I became vividly aware of the differences in our energies. I wrote endlessly about relationships and many letters to Gerry, some I gave him, some I did not. I became vividly aware that we had a relationship problem and I felt determined at that point, to find a solution.

After a period of months, attending Tony twice a week, he invited me to join a small spiritual development group he was facilitating, so I attended the group once a week and cut down my healing sessions to one a week also. When Christmas came Tony asked us to write down our New Years goals and ideals and all excited I arrived at the group night, ready to share. It was not long before I felt like the alien again. Most people in the group had down to earth ideals like, a new washing machine, more meditation/relaxation time, or a regular night out with their partner. My ideals were, akin to, unity and oneness with my higher self, balance of body mind and spirit and expression of the highest form of divine love in the Earth. One group member had a variation of one of my goals, but overall I was speaking a different language and felt outside and different. Tony smiled his little smile and said nothing.

Around this time, I began to understand the nun phobia and was feeling a strong desire to become a healer, but keeping the desire hidden, as I felt totally unworthy of being a healer. Who did I think I was? Up to then, I had dabbled in a number of possible career outlets but now I realised I had very strong and definite spiritual ideals. I had huge expectations of myself in the Earth and a passionate dream to be a healing channel and spiritual teacher. I was reading three or four spiritual and other development books at a time and I studied, wrote and meditated relentlessly. I had found my passion, one I had been seeking for many years and all that stood in my way, was a mountainous sense of unworthiness. Tony would say to me – do you not know who you are? I would look at him as if he were speaking Chinese, as I felt weak, imperfect, unworthy and so vulnerable in the Earth. I was learning to survive and find myself, but I did not feel remotely powerful or confident. He told me I was one of 'The Essenes' in a past life ('The Essenes' were followers of a religious way of living in Judaism that flourished from 2nd. Century B.C. to 1st. Century A.D.) and that I had lived many lives as a healer and in religious life. None of this penetrated my being. It was enough that he believed in me, encouraged me and was teaching me survival skills.

Tony encouraged me to visualise for what I was seeking and later I learnt how to transform things in my life through visualisation. Much like the children's transformer toys where a robot becomes a car, one can transform fear images and real life stressful happenings by seeing something different in ones mind. The mind is like a drawing board and a seed of thought sown in the mind can be fed through visualisation and positive imagining and be born into the Earth in time.

Everything begins as a thought in the mind first. It is those thoughts we feed in a positive way that bear fruit. If we can't imagine it or see it in our minds eye, then it won't happen. A good example of this is - a woman who attended a Christmas meditation evening I hosted. I asked the group to visualise and imagine receiving something they really wanted, but never allowed themselves to have, or reach for. The following year at the same event this woman stood up and said, a miracle happened for her after that night. Her daughter lived in America and living alone, she missed her desperately, but she could never afford to visit, so she never allowed herself to dream of, or imagine going. That night she began visualising herself at the airport, arriving in America and being with her daughter. A neighbour called to the door sometime later and gifted her, an airline ticket to the States and everything else she needed for her journey was gifted to her also. There were stars dancing in her eyes as she told us the story. The universe answered her prayer, so we need to ask heaven, our guides and angels for what it is we are seeking and then we need to visualise and imagine receiving it. What we ask for does not always come packaged in the way we imagine, but what comes carries the essence of what we are seeking.

My first visualisation experience was a fun one. I needed clothes so I visualised buying something new, putting it in my wardrobe and wearing it and before long I won a £100 voucher. It felt like a little piece of magic. It is the long term dreams we feed and visualise on that can take time, patience and dedication, as they may take many years to manifest fully, as there are often many things to learn along the way, to ready ourselves for the dream in its entirety. When we become despondent, flat and disappointed, it is helpful to express those feelings and have a cry, then to look at how far we have come along the road of that dream, a little like watching the petals of a flower open one by one. Each opening, just like each part of the dream, has a magic of its own. Experience the joy of each new step along the way and know that once you can see the dream fully birthed in your mind's eye, when the time is divinely right and you are ready, it will be born into the Earth. This is the law of the universe.

At another time, a client came that was grieving and broken hearted, because her long term dream of giving birth to a baby had resulted in numerous miscarriages. While we were working with the grief, she became pregnant and at around the time she had lost the other babies, she started to have the same horrific dreams that preceded miscarriage. Each time she had one of these dreams, we journeyed into the dream through meditation and visualised taking control, changing the images and healing the dream so the outcome was what she desired. These dreams represented fears and mental attitude patterns she was working with in her life. We did these healing journeys a number of times and this woman gave birth to a healthy baby boy. A very exciting miracle, I felt blessed to watch.

Shortly after I became aware of my healing passion, I made an appointment to see Austin Byrne, who is gifted in the areas of astrology, astronomy and spiritual teaching. Without knowing anything about me other than my birth date, time and place, he did an astrological chart and tape, outlining my gifts, talents and possible work arenas, which included healing and he also looked at relationships and other areas of my life. This reading cemented my passion to become a healer and I shared my private dream with someone for the first time. Austin was hugely encouraging and supportive and put me in touch with Lilla Bek of the National Federation of Spiritual Healers in the United

Kingdom. Lilla was a leading light in this worldwide organisation at that time, and she was very supportive, sponsoring me to enrol as a probationer healer. She is a very gifted healer, spiritual teacher, sacred mathematician, psychic reader and author of a number of spiritual books. I began to attend Lilla's weekend workshops in Ireland as part of my training.

Austin also told me to work on the relationship with my Mam as it needed healing; something I thought was not possible, because she was dead. He said it could be healed and attended to, no matter where she was. Later, I understood that those we are linked corded or connected to, are joined to us by an invisible cord, or beam of energy, just like an umbilical cord and no matter where either person goes in the universe, that cord of energy remains connected. It can be in a healthy or unhealthy state, but we can heal it at any time, changing it into a radiant healthy cord. I wrote to my Mam and a whole lot of anger, hurt and pain poured out, combined with an awful lot of tears and sadness. I gave myself permission to empty all my feelings onto paper and only then could I see all that was precious, that she had gifted me. The next step I took was to write a letter of forgiveness to her and I thanked her for all she had given me. I could now see her humanness and knew that she gave me all that she knew, all she was capable of, at that time. Our parents are human after all, learning and growing in the earth, just as we are. A load had lifted from my heart and soul. A few nights later, I had a very vivid dream, where my Mam was giving birth and I was assisting her and looking after her while the baby was being born. After the birth, she put her arms around me, thanked me and told me that she really loved me. That dream and the work I did changed everything with her. I woke up crying with joy, as she had never before told me she loved me. I spent my life wanting to be good enough for her love and feeling I never measured up. The feeling in that dream was divine and has stayed with me all these years later.

This is just one of the many issues in my life I began to seek healing for, expressing myself through writing, artwork and meditation. I wrote about my childhood, schooling, pregnancies, relationship, compassion, hope, possibility and everyday life and I felt somehow guided as I wrote and began to find answers to many of my questions.

Healing with Tony continued for two years. After the first year, though I felt more solid, healthy and able to cope, I was still quite scared of myself and reverting back to where I had come from – a fate worse than death. I was in the middle of processing a body of work and it felt a little like being a toddler who was learning to walk, but having to return to Mum for comfort and support on a regular basis.

I immersed myself at this time in writing, reading, meditating and studying anything and everything I could find that explored the arena of spiritual/emotional development and healing. I was quite fanatical for some time, as you are, when something has saved your life. The fanaticism served it's purpose, as it supported me to fully recognise my spiritual passion and dream and it encouraged me to express, clear and process all that had happened to me, clearing the pathway for the realisation of my dream. There are often many layers of learning attached to some of our experiences and we can only deal with the layer that is presented to us, at a given time. It is a good thing that our psyche somehow regulates a layered process of evolvement, through our learning experiences. The bulk of the processing and healing I needed to do with my Mother was done, but every now and then another little piece rears its head and I need to write and cry once more, sometimes after a moments tears these feelings pass. When we experience these moments, wisps of old pain and sadness are leaving our bodies.

I made a number of return visits to Austin Byrne for guidance and support and I spoke to him about how I was now aware that I was tuning into a lot of thoughts and feelings, (that were not mine) when I was with other people. I did not fully understand what was happening, how to deal with it or what to do with it. Austin sent me to a spiritual medium, who I think was Irish but resident in the U.K., to ask if I could join a developing circle, to develop my mediumship abilities. I was surprised I had any of those and was quite terrified of the word 'psychic' and of spirits appearing to me. I attended an evening given by this man for the public, approached him afterwards and asked could I join a developing circle. He looked at me in amazement, said "it's already developed my dear" and then he walked away, leaving me looking after him, with open mouthed shock. This man was telling me I had this ability, that I did not know I had until recently, already developed, the very self same ability, that had me fearful I had a mental problem all my life. Yes, I was hugely sensitive and felt things instantly when I met someone or walked into a room. I knew if people were telling me one thing and thinking something else. I knew if they had reactions or attitudes to this or that. I had heard people thinking since I was a small child and I thought I was nuts. Now that I was expressing and emptying a lot of my own feelings, I was more aware of what I was picking up and I began the journey through meditation, writing and study, that taught me to trust and interpret what I was tuning into.

Now I realise that some lens in my energy scans people on a very unconscious level and only when I am asked, do I seek to interpret it and bring it into my consciousness.

As I learnt to meditate and express my feelings, I learnt to calm my mind, give it rest spaces, let go and empty myself. This made it easier for me to let go the psychic (meaning of the soul) imprints or information about a person that I pick up. When I spend a long time in the company of others, I can feel quite upset and confused, unless I am taking regular time to empty all that fills me, as I unconsciously tune into others. I have tried turning off this ability, but don't seem to be able to, so I seek to understand it and work with it instead.

Meditation is fascinating. It is really interacting with the universal or spiritual light or energy that we are created from and that we need for health and wellbeing. So meditation is needed for refuelling our bodies. Thirty minutes meditation is the most efficient way of re-energising ourselves. When we are busy and interacting with all the demands of a hectic life, that incorporates our own emotional/spiritual growth and development, our cells and organs become tight and tense and we are no longer refuelling efficiently, so we become tired, irritable and stressed.

A simple meditation for example, (that can be done with our eyes closed sitting or lying), is seeing a bud open slowly into a flower, in our body centres (head/throat/heart/tummy), which relaxes us, calms our minds and opens our cells and organs to receive the energy that is all around us, giving valuable time for us to re-energise and the body and mind to recover. There are endless images one can use to do this simple exercise. The aim is to stop doing, sit or lie, open the cells and organs by using simple imagery and absorb like a sponge that energy that is in abundance around us. Practice makes perfect. The universal light or creative light has miraculous properties. It carries energy, wisdom, knowledge, support, encouragement and healing, into our bodies and minds. It will in the future be fully and completely scientifically interpreted I am sure. It is a natural resource that is undervalued and underused in our society at this time and could gift us endless treasures, if we were to utilise it fully.

Meditation on another level, can take us on journeys into our own cell memories, to uncover wisdom we have gathered from past lifetimes. It can also help to identify and release old hurts and pains, so we may empty and heal. When the energy of light or meditation begins to flow through us, it supports the efficient release of old feelings, old cells, old relationships and attitudes, old parts of our lives and anything we no longer need to carry.

Meditation links us to the spirit world, to those we love who have gone there, to our spiritual guides, angels and heavenly support system and it takes us into the arms of our spiritual team in the heavens.

Meditation uncovers our dreams, passions and true potential and links us with the creative power that is within each of us. It is hugely empowering. As Nelson Mandela famously said in his inaugural speech – 'it is our power that we are most afraid of'.

Meditation guides us, step by step, to uncover, step into and own, our own power, not a power or control over others, but a unique individual creative power that is in each of us, a recognition of who we are. We are powerful beyond measure.

On a meditative journey I undertook myself; I understood the 'nun phobia' I had experienced. I had spent a number of past lifetimes in religious life and though I had gathered a lot of spiritual wisdom, I had hugely denied my other needs and sacrificed my physical body. So yes, I felt a huge pull to the spiritual ideal I had chosen to embody in this lifetime, but also the terror that I would sacrifice myself again, or be trapped or imprisoned somewhere, like I had felt in the convent in a past life. As I understood this and committed to clearing old sacrifice patterns, so I could live my life and dreams without sacrificing any of my needs, little by little, the fear disappeared. Clarity and emotional and spiritual education is vital in our lives.

Chapter 7

Moving On

I don't know what it is about Wednesday's, but it is a day that I tend to write endlessly. So, I had found my spiritual passion and dream, continuing to develop and grow, emotionally, physically and spiritually in every way that I could. All that I was learning was of great benefit to my children.

From the moment I stopped breastfeeding Davin and started giving him 'cow milk formula', he began to experience constipation, colds, chest infections and croup. Every month, the doctor gave him an antibiotic over the course of about a year and often, at night time, I would sit steaming up his room, when he could not breathe and a horrendous sound would come from his chest and throat. Eventually he was given 'Ventolin' an asthmatic drug. Shortly after he was prescribed 'Ventolin', I had a bad bout of bronchitis and deciding to try it, I was shocked to find my body shaking like a leaf, for some time afterwards. Having observed the positive effect a change of diet had on my system and not wanting my toddler to be taking this drug, I decided to explore a change of diet with him. Little by little I discovered the foods that triggered off this reaction in his body. His system had a huge reaction to dairy foods, so I introduced Soya milk that had been sweetened with apply juice concentrate, lots of fruit and vegetables and very little sugar. My gorgeous little babe made a wonderful recovery and all medication ceased. Subsequently I had him allergy tested and the triggers I had observed were all highlighted. When he would go to a birthday party, I would feed him dinner in advance, in the hope that he would not be able to eat too much sugar, dairy, colouring, preservatives, additives and sweetened fizzy drinks. Many times he came back from a party wheezing and having difficulty breathing and he would ask for cider vinegar and juice as it supported the rebalancing of his system and he recognised that, even as a small child. As an adult, he tends towards healthy foods. People around me were not very supportive about his dietary change at first, but I knew it worked and I was no longer experiencing the terror of my child unable to breathe freely and that was an enormous relief. However, I kept 'Ventolin' in the press, just in case. Luckily I never had to use it.

A lot has been written about allergic reactions to food and I don't think all allergic reactions are written in stone, or affect us throughout the entire course of our lives. For example dairy fills me with muscous and I tend towards sinus in the winter months when it is damp and wet in Ireland, but when I am in a dry warm country or in summertime, my system seems to cope much better with it. One can be allergic to chocolate for example for a period and then that reaction can disappear entirely. So, what we can experience at a given time in our lives, are food sensitivities or allergic reactions that can be present or disappear, depending upon our sensitivity, environment or what we are dealing with physically and emotionally, in our bodies and lives.

Organic food and foods next to nature are more in tune with the vibration of our cells and the clear spiritual rhythm of natural food, that has not been unduly coloured, processed or added to, sits in harmony with the spiritual rhythm of our cells. People that are processing a lot emotionally and people that are very sensitive, tend to have more immediate and obvious allergic reactions to food and drink. However, a bit of what you fancy does you good (something I have to add due to my sweet tooth) and we are capable of clearing and transforming any reaction we may experience, when we deviate, every now and then, from a 'next to nature' diet. There are a number of people who have 'life threatening' allergic reactions to nuts for example, but thankfully this is not the norm. There is nothing like a day or two on fruit, vegetables, water and homemade soups to clean the system.

During this time of study and development, I stopped taking all medication and I discovered, that by using diet, meditation, exercise and emotional processing I could at all times, support my body's natural movement towards health and wellbeing. A lot of physical ailments that had plagued me disappeared and luckily I no longer needed medical drugs. Apart from the odd tooth anaesthetic, I live my life without medication of any sort and seek to rebalance my body naturally, incorporating natural treatments that work with the body's energy, like acupuncture, reflexology, aromatherapy massage, flower essences and sometimes homeopathy.

It is fair to say that we often crave what we are allergic to and Davin at one point would only eat what he was allergic to, which resulted in his skin breaking out in eczema patches. At this point, Tony advised me to remove the offending foods, allow him to be hungry and he would eventually eat. My children never tire of reminding me of the awful things I did, like reheating Davin's dinner for breakfast, a number of times, or insisting they eat one of the two brussel sprouts on their plates! The tactic, however awful, worked. For the most part after that, I reared my kids without drugs or medication and a fruit and juice day, incorporating healthy soups, were the order of the day, if they had a cold or flu.

Part of my dietary change was that I decided I would stop eating meat and become vegetarian, to see if my health improved further and being a bit fanatical and all or nothing at that time, I just stopped eating meat one day. During the following six months, I became very ill twice as my body released the residues of meat as I adjusted to my new diet. My aunt wanted to have me hospitalised I was so ill, but I insisted on 'cold turkey' and hey I survived and never looked back. I am the variety of new age vegetarian that eats fish from time to time and personally I feel very healthy eating in that way, but I acknowledge that diet is a very personal thing and many people, feel the need for meat in their diets. My children were and still are meat eaters as I did not feel qualified enough to rear them as vegetarians. Food gives me great pleasure, but I would advise if you are making a dietary change, to do it more slowly and gently, as it is easier on the system. My way is not the high way in this case!

As I followed my newfound path, my Dad's 'Parkinson's disease' and angina were deteriorating and I worried a lot, in case he would fall down the stairs or become ill, when no one was with him. Many times I asked him to come and live with us, but he liked his independence and did not want to disturb my family life or be a burden. Though the boys and I went to visit him two or three times a week and we talked every day on the phone, I was very concerned about him. Tony Hogan did a thing called 'absent healing', while during meditation, he would concentrate on sending light, love and healing rays to a person. I signed my Dad up for this spiritual support.

It was coming close to two years since I began working with Tony. I was developing fast as a probationer healer, still very sensitive but now had the tools to work with that sensitivity and my development, in a very effective way. A series of events led to Tony, telling me he could do no more for me. He realised that I could now interpret, to a degree, what I was tuning into and it was time for me, to put into action all that I had learned. So, it was time for me to go it alone, as it were. I was terrified and thought I would disintegrate and die without those two visits to Tony a week. I no longer needed the umbilical cord and was breathing without it, but the realisation had not dawned on me. The birth into my chosen spiritual journey was complete and after a while, terror gave way to action and I continued to practice all I had learned and I survived breathing on my own.

Tony died a few years ago and though I felt shocked when I heard it, as he was still a relatively young man, the deepest gratitude and love for this man, who was, my mentor, teacher, lifeline and friend awoke inside me. He knew when I needed to fly and let me go, despite the deep bond of friendship than grew between us. He has come from spirit a number of times since to support me. Tony, I am immeasurably grateful to you, for guiding the birthing of me into my body and spiritual dream and words could never adequately express the depth of my gratitude. I had a vivid and amazing dream once where he gifted me gold, frankincense and myrrh. He was and still is in spirit, a most amazing and brilliant healer and his dedication to his gift and support of people was awe inspiring. Tony, thank you for everything you gifted me. I trust I am a credit to you.

Tony, like my father was a powerful influence in my life. It was about six months away from my thirtieth birthday, close to the end of my Saturn return and I had changed dramatically. The time had come to tell my Dad that I was a practising healer. I felt very nervous telling him, as 'healing' and 'healers' were thin on the ground in Ireland in 1985 and were viewed by many as weird and strange, and though healing, spiritual and psychic pursuits were ridiculed and criticised by many, my Dad seemed fine about it.

Shortly after I spoke to my Dad, my Mother came to me in a dream, to tell me, my Dad had died and while I was hysterical in the dream, she sat with me, soothing me and telling me all would be okay. Dreams are open to interpretation and I had been studying my dreams and the individual language of dream interpretation for some time, often waking after a dream in the middle of the night and recording it in my journal, so I would not forget it. I sought to interpret my dreams intuitively but guided always by my bible of the time, 'Dreams your magic mirror', by Edgar Cayce. This particular dream left me wondering if my father was close to death, or if it just represented a big change I was making. Death so often in our dreams just represents a rebirth we are making in our own development, so it felt easier to accept this interpretation. However, I was increasingly worried about my Dad and Christmas day of 1985 was the first Christmas he had not cried for my Mam, since her death.

I was planning a New Year's eve party in my home in Co. Meath and on the night of the thirtieth of December 1985, I dreamt that I was at the party and a call came for me to go to the hospital as my Father had been admitted, but when I arrived there I was too late and he had already died. I awoke, on New Year's Eve, three months before my thirtieth birthday, cancelled the party and drove with the boys to my Dad's home. My sister Marian also arrived with her two little girls and my younger brother Eanna was also there. I encouraged my Dad to have his favourite smoked mackerel, brown bread and a piece of my aunt Carmel's Christmas cake. Also, I returned twenty pounds I had borrowed from him, despite his protests and unwillingness to take it back, and his comment that I was just like my Mother, who insisted on paying back anything she owed. The strange thing was he put the twenty pounds in his trouser pocket, not his wallet, as he would always have done.

Shortly after eating, he got a pain in his chest. I was instantly alarmed, even though he said it was his usual angina attack. He went towards the stairs to get his pills and I climbed behind him, in case he would fall backwards. He lay down on the bed as the pain became very severe and he was entering the throes of a major heart attack. An oily sweat broke out on his forehead and he could barely speak. He told me to take off his shoes and open his shirt and tie. I called my brother Eanna and asked him to call an ambulance. My Dad said "no ambulance", which was something we ignored, as he did not want to go to hospital even though he was in this desperate pain. Quite rapidly, he was in agony, unable to speak but fully conscious.

I found myself doing what I was trained to do, putting my hands on him and concentrating on pouring light, love and healing into his body. After what seemed like forever, the ambulance arrived. I was screaming inside for help for him, as it was so hard to watch him in this agony. Another part of me had a role to fulfil and I kept focusing on sending him healing until the ambulance men complete with stretcher and oxygen arrived.

I took my hands away from my Dad's body and he instantly turned purple, unable to breathe. He had been breathing through my hands and if I could have given him my heart and lungs I would have. I only understood the significance of this happening, months later. The oxygen brought colour back to his face. I went with him in the ambulance, my sister stayed to mind the children and my brother followed in the car.

My Dad was dying and the ambulance at breakneck speed was rushing to try and save his life. I held him and his eyes never left mine as if he was drinking me in, and he tried so very hard through the oxygen mask to tell me something. I told him he could tell me later, but I knew there would be no later. The ambulance reversed to the door and a team of doctors waited to try and save my Father. I took my hands and eyes away from him and stood back, discovering afterwards that he died in the five paces it took, to reach the medical team. My knight in shining armour had died and I hoped my newfound healing touch supported and comforted him on his journey.

I could not have asked for more in a Father. I adored him and he adored me. Thank you, my very loving Dad for your endless love and patience with a very sensitive and easily scared little girl. What he gave me was immeasurable. I would not have survived as a 'sensitive' in the world, without his love. The blanket of his complete protection and love was always wrapped around me and I believe still is. My difference, though he may not have been able to put words on it, caused him instinctively to protect me. There was a beautiful smell, like roses, emanating from his body after he died. I like to think it was the divine love he had bathed us in all his life, gifted back to him by those who received him in spirit. When the hospital returned his clothes to me, the twenty pounds was in his pocket, his final gift to me.

During the preparation for my Father's funeral, his family from Cape Clear Island, West Cork arrived and the dam of sadness and loss burst in me. I could hear his voice, smell his beloved ocean, see his face in theirs and feel the softness of his energy radiating through them. I sat on the stairs of my childhood home and howled like a wounded cub. Yes, I was happy to let him go home, but I would miss him so badly. He had gifted me enough love to last me a hundred lifetimes. That night he died, I crawled into his bed, sleeping just where he last lay when he had the heart attack and Gerry slept beside me. I slept like a baby, the only one who slept well in the house. I guess I was wrapped in the comfort of his smell and residual energy he had left in that bed. He came to Gerry in a dream that night and held up his left hand, to show us it was no longer shaking from the Parkinson's disease. He was well again. He had a garda (Irish Police) escort to the church and as he was a dedicated and wonderful teacher, the principal of a large boy's school for many years, a vast sea of people came to honour him and say goodbye.

It took a lot of persuasion, to get me, to go back to my home in Co. Meath. It takes a while after someone dies to catch up with their absence and for a long time after, when the phone rang, I would think it was him. I was not able to sleep properly for some time afterwards and asked heaven what was wrong? My Father came to me in a dream and as we were sitting having a cup of tea, he started to turn bright purple and I was terrified. He stayed with me in the dream until my terror passed and I could see that he was happy and well. After I woke, I understood why I had not been sleeping, as the shock of seeing him, turn purple the day he died, had lodged in my body and terrified me. He came to teach me, just as he had always explained things to me, when I felt scared or confused.

The greatest gift of that time was that my Father proved to me that I was a healer, as the life force coming through my hands, supported him to breathe and he only turned purple when I removed my hands. Also, he died in the ambulance, the moment I took my hands away from his body. Healing supports people on their journeys. It does not keep them alive no matter what, rather supports them wherever they need to go. I hope it made his passing, gentler and a little easier. I got the proof I had been seeking in a very unusual way. Up to then, I had a deep desire to become a healer but I never thought I would be capable, worthy or good enough.

When a parent or someone close dies, it represents something precious in our growth and development, like a reflection in a mirror, a door opening to the next stage of our spiritual journey. Those who love us never truly leave us. They just leave their bodies but are corded or connected to us forever. They take us with them in some way into the spirit world and deeper into our own spiritual journey.

Mothers, reflect how we mother ourselves and when my Mother died, I began the process of mothering my boys and through that; the process of nurturing and mothering myself, began. So, my Mothers death reflected and represented a powerful turning point in my life.

Fathers, reflect how we express ourselves in the World. When my Father died, I was beginning my journey as a healer and teacher in the Earth. So, his death represented a powerful opening into life, expressing my soul passion and dream.

If I look at why my Dad, suffered Parkinson's disease, I have to look at the central nervous system, where it originates. The central nervous system is the home of the emotional body and when there are deep emotional shocks, they lodge in the central nervous system, waiting to be processed. If they are not processed in someway, shock after shock can overload the system and cause it to malfunction, thereby affecting the functions in the body that the central nervous system, govern. My Dad's sister died in childbirth and he helped rear her child. I never heard him speak about the loss of her. His Mother died when he was quite young and he was very close to her. He never spoke about that either. It was after his Father's death that he was diagnosed with Parkinson's disease and he had some issues with his Father,

I don't think he resolved in this life. Also, my Father got a terrible shock as a young man, home one summer from teacher training college. He was working in his Father's fishing boat and somehow fell between two boats. The boats closed over, trapping him and he was unconscious by the time he was lifted from the water. The shock from this accident would have lodged in his body, possibly setting the precedent for all the other emotional shocks to follow. There was no language or facility for processing in those days, so a lifelong habit ensued. My Father's body shook and shuddered with Parkinson's and the huge effort it took to hold all these shocks and emotions in his body. His first breath was to provide a comfortable home and good standard of living for his wife and children. His emotional body was left to one side and perhaps he was unaware of those emotional shocks inside him. My Mother on the other hand, I think was aware of her feelings and fought to keep them under control, which explains to me how their illnesses manifested through different organs.

This is the era of developing, expressing and understanding the emotional body and how it affects our physical function. It is the era of owning, honouring and getting to know our physical bodies and all that manifests through them, like our emotions, soul dreams and desires. For optimum health and wellbeing, we need to spend more time understanding the functions and interaction of the body, mind-emotions and soul, and devise a way of bringing this new found awareness and understanding into mainstream education. This type of awareness and education will in time become the opium of the masses. It is the next logical step to health and wellbeing.

My parents died when I was relatively young and there was a lot of grief and a sense of losing my childhood family space, quite rapidly. This left me with a freedom in one sense, of being able to live life on my terms, without having to negotiate my way through my parent's attitudes or expectations of me, as I was fast becoming a very different person, in my expression and thinking, to that of my childhood and extended family. In another sense, I was left with a fear of loss, a fear of losing everyone I knew and loved.

Three months after my Dad's death, on ninth March 1986, the day of my thirtieth birthday, I was standing in Co. Clare watching the burial of my maternal grandfather Joe, the only grandparent who I had shared the thirty years of my life with. I think I was numb at that stage as three important men had left my life, in one way or another, over a six month period. It reflected a major change I was making in my outer expression in the World. My Granda Joe was a hardworking man, the boss in the house, very strict with his children but with his grandchildren he was very amenable and gentle. Time and experience had mellowed him. During the summers, we worked alongside him, making hay, serving petrol and foodstuff, in his shop. His gratitude was gifted to us in the form of a fresh cream cake or a handful of sweets or chocolate. For some reason he always kept a picture of me in my Communion dress on his dresser.

Chapter 8

Healing Rays

The death of my Father and Grandfather heralded the beginning of my healing work. I was a probationer healing member of the 'National Federation of Spiritual Healers', a worldwide organisation, based in the United Kingdom, in 1986, and took my first tentative steps towards working with clients. There were people whose homes I visited and those who I sent healing, love and light to, during a meditative state, from my own home. In those days, people generally requested healing, only when they had exhausted all avenues of medical science. In the early days, I stood in silence, lightly touching the head, heart and stomach of a person and concentrating mentally on radiating white healing light into their bodies and lives.

Spiritual healing focuses on the spiritual centres of an individual, those centres that align with the endocrine glands in the physical body. The initial response people had, was a feeling of calmness, peace and deep relaxation, some people finding it easier to mentally let go, than others. I noticed after a session, that people's eyes danced with light and they looked new born in some way. At the beginning, my confidence was not very high, so I concentrated on doing the sessions and hoping for the best. Over many years, I have learnt, that doing a healing session with someone, is giving a gift of all, that spiritual light and energy offers and just like any other gift, what the free will and creative consciousness of that individual does with it, is entirely up to them.

It is the job of the healer, to gift the light of healing, then let go and know the manifestation of the healing, will become what the person most needs and that decision is made by a persons inner creative and body consciousness.

I travelled from house to house working with children and adults alike and watched healing support asthmatic children, who were on maximum medication, breathe more calmly and easily. By adulthood, these children had recovered fully and joining with medical science, healing supported the maintenance of the moment, these children needed, at that time. I watched healing support adults to relax de-stress and cope more effectively with life, difficult relationships, bereavement and so forth. It brought them a new found self belief and confidence and supported them to change their lives in positive and productive ways. Not having been blessed with an overdose of confidence, I was relieved it was working in some form or other.

In the early days of doing healing, Kenn aged six and now at school developed warts, some fifty of them on his hands, face and other parts of his body. I tried everything, from medical preparations and cryosurgery to holy wells, dandelion milk and drinking nettle tea (the poor child), but nothing worked. The doctor had never seen a case of this magnitude, so Kenn was scheduled for surgery but I was warned that he would have scars. Desperately, I turned to healing. Strangely, I had not thought to try it, up to that point and I had nothing to lose. Each night, when Kenn fell asleep on his top bunk bed, I would tiptoe into his room, place my hands on his head and tummy, visualise filling his body with white light while silently talking to him and showing him mental pictures of me taking him to meet his Grandad in the garden of heaven, where he handed his warts, one by one to his Grandad, who transformed them into flowers and planted them in his heavenly garden. In five days, every wart had disappeared from Kenn's body. His teachers could not believe it and repeatedly asked him what cream I rubbed on. He kept repeating to them that I did healing on them. Kenn was speaking a foreign language to them as healing was far from the norm. I was as amazed as the teachers, as I watched the miracle of his warts just melting away. This gave me the confidence I needed to work with the children, whenever they were ill.

I have always seen myself as a healing channel, one who facilitates the flow of an abundance of divine love and healing light into the Earth, not the one who does the healing, more the one who facilitates the gifting of the light that manifests the healing. From the moment

I aligned myself with the dream of becoming a healer, I signed a contract so to speak, to process, on an ongoing basis, my emotional and physical body, so I could be a healthy open pathway for this energy. It is vital that every healer learns to process anything 'sticky' in the body that has been held over a period of time. Processing teaches us the art of emptying and letting go and while this is vital for health and wellbeing, it is doubly vital when one is a healer.

Payment and healing has long been debated, some thinking that no money should change hands as healing is a gift from God. My thinking is that all our unique individual gifts, no matter how they manifest, are God given and that we live on this Earth and money is the currency, so an exchange of your gifts and talents for an agreed fee, is a perfectly balanced and normal way of doing business, as one does, more often than not, need to earn a living. However, in the early days, I received all manner of amusing payments, ranging from Johnson and Johnson baby products, to a roll of waxed bread wrapping paper, to a cup of tea and a sandwich or five pounds to cover my petrol expenses. Whatever the payment, I was happy and being a probationer healer, thrilled with the opportunity of practicing my passion and dream.

In life, we all need acknowledgement and to see the results of our work. Sometimes, in the healing field, ones work is not always visible, in immediate earthy terms. When my time came to work with people with terminal cancer or central nervous system illnesses for example, I would observe the person experiencing a calm, relaxed state during the healing, but at times could not see any obvious long term effect or changes in their health. I came to understand that just like everything in nature grows beneath the ground or within itself first, we all grow and change deep within our hidden selves too, before the result is birthed into the Earth and sometimes that result is not born until we enter the spirit world or in the next lifetime. Supporting someone on their journey, what ever that is, is what I do.

The acknowledgement can come in observing someone experiencing a peaceful relaxed state for half an hour or seeing a mental and emotional strength awaken in them, that enables them deal more effectively with their terminal illness or hearing a client say they feel a burden they have carried emotionally or physically for many years has been lifted or disappeared. Then, there is the acknowledgement that comes from watching someone who has been in the tremendous pain and restricted movement of arthritis since childhood, recover completely. In this case, the doctor said it must have been a mis-diagnosis, we can't find any trace of arthritis in your body now, despite the fact that it was diagnosed and treated medically for many years. How I love the miracle of spirit that confounds logic and medical science, as we know it today.

My primary role was still rearing the boys and healing sessions I scheduled around the times, they were at school or the odd evening Gerry was available to mind them. I was playing basketball again, accompanied by the boys, walking Cas, the wonderful, wild Dalmatian that became one of my charges for a while and all the time I continued to work incessantly with myself and my emotional, mental, spiritual and physical development. The more meditation, dream work, processing, emotional and spiritual development I did, the wider the gulf became between Gerry and I. My understanding of karma at that time, (the unfinished business we take to the Earth from past lifetimes), was, that I had to get this relationship to work, so I went for guidance, wrote about it, wrote to Gerry, visualised, meditated, the lot. Nothing seemed to bear fruit. We were in two different worlds, on two different wavelengths and in fairness to Gerry, I had changed dramatically, from the person he initially met. My needs were now very different and I craved, emotional and spiritual communication, companionship and support.

While the spirit world was supporting me after my time with Tony Hogan ended, there was no one I could turn to, for this type of nurturing. I did not know who I was, when I married Gerry and maybe the average twenty two year old, has not uncovered who they are at that stage, so I was not unusual in this. Also, the depth to which I had uncovered my emotional self and my unusual passions and dreams (all necessary training for the journey ahead), awoke in me a deep need to communicate with like minded people. I began to meditate and visualise on making soul connections with like minded people, as I pretty much felt all alone inside. Of course, the precious love of my sister Marian, brothers Eanna and Barry and many friends and family were around me, but inside I was alone and I did not know how to share all this inner stuff and I was also protecting myself, as deep feelings were hidden in my family and generally at that time and spiritual 'mumbo jumbo' dismissed. I did not want to risk the loss or possible judgement of those around me.

As we lived out in the country, everywhere the children, Gerry or I went, involved a lot of driving, so we made a decision to move to the city in 1987. Our home sold very quickly and we invested in an old two storey over basement property, needing renovation in Phibsboro, Dublin. I discovered a wonderful, tiny, multi-denominational school for the boys and while it was a big adjustment for them, they were very happy there, embraced by the small family like community of the school. I explained to the boys that there were new friends waiting to meet them, friends they had agreed to meet, as part of their journey through life, known to them from past lifetimes. Kenn was nine and Davin was seven when we said goodbye to the beautiful home Gerry had designed for us. I felt very sad leaving this home and the rolling hills and green meadows, where I had meandered regularly, breathing the clear air of the countryside. Also, I had many loving friends, who I may not have shared my innermost thoughts with, but who loved and cherished me nonetheless.

My brother Eanna, who was now the owner of what was originally our family home, gifted us a roof over our heads, while the house was being renovated. Gerry busied himself with the huge job of this house renovation. The boys settled happily at school and I met some like minded friends. I liked being back in my parents home, close to my brother, and the feeling that a blanket of family love was around me. Life seemed to settle for a while. On one level, I was more content, but there was turmoil underneath that whispered things I did not want to hear.

Eventually, we moved into the new house, that Gerry had lovingly and painstakingly renovated and the new kitchen in the basement was all that I dreamed of. I continued for a while ignoring the whispers, until one day a bird flew in and got trapped in one of the bedrooms and I knew that bird was me. The penny dropped and I realised that karma was not about staying in a relationship no matter what, it was about setting oneself free. I needed to leave my relationship with Gerry and fly free. In my consciousness, I had left no stone unturned in exploring the relationship. My needs were now very different, to those of an innocent young woman starting out in life and a fork on my spiritual road had taken me in a very different direction to Gerry. At this point, the relationship has ceased to nurture either of us.

I like Lilla Bek's interpretation of relationship, which is, that we meet someone with a colour we need and we have a colour they need, and when the exchange is done, the contract is over and we say thank you and journey on. Colours represent the many ways we express ourselves in the Earth. Gerry is a passionate, totally committed and very brilliant architect and I feel he gifted me, apart from our beautiful boys, the colour that supported me to awaken to the huge passion of my own dream, as it was within my marriage, that the realisation of the dream awoke in me. It was like a womb space, out of which the real me was birthed. For Gerry too, there was a colour he needed that I gifted him and may it support him, with whatever his soul needs to express.

I then did something I am not very proud of. I have always been very afraid of serious confrontation and possible aggression, so I ran away and left Gerry a note. I am ashamed I left that way. Today I would do it very differently, but it was where I was at, at the time and I was very frightened. I can but say, I am very sorry Gerry that I did the leaving in that way, forgive myself and move on. What we term mistakes are part and parcel of the human condition of growth and development and the choices we make at a given time, are based on our level of consciousness at that time. It took quite some time, before things were resolved between us and naturally Gerry was very hurt and angry at the time, because I had made the decision to separate. I questioned myself on this decision a thousand times, but eventually I had to stop, as I knew in my heart, we were on two different pathways.

Eventually, we got a legal separation, as divorce was not available in Ireland at the time, divided our home, organised our finances and set about learning how to live independently of each other. The end of a marriage is like a death, no matter who makes the decision to separate and there is a grieving process, as your life is reborn again. I do believe, if a relationship is over for one person, then it is also over for the other, even though it may take them some time to recognise that. I resent the term 'relationship failure', as in my consciousness, there is no such thing. All relationships have a purpose and a lifespan, whether that be, ten months, ten years or a lifetime. Even a month spent sharing your love and time with another, is a valuable, precious space of growth and development. The love and energy we exchange in relationship, supports us to grow, develop and express who we are in the Earth. I encouraged, supported, pushed and prodded Gerry, to move into private practice as I so believed in his ability and his dream.

I want to thank you Gerry, for so much, two gorgeous sons who I love with all my heart, a bridge that we crossed together as we entered the adult world of grown-up-ness and home owning, your hard and dedicated work that financially supported our home, the colour of your passion and dream that supported me to awaken to my own dream, a space for me to learn and grow, our beautiful home you designed and thank you for the love you felt able to gift me over ten years of marriage.

I know I also gifted Gerry, his two sons, who he loves with all his heart and the many different manifestations, of all the love I felt able to give, every day of our journey together. Nowadays, when we meet, there is a calm, loving, respectful gentleness, between us I am deeply grateful for.

In following my heart and knowing the relationship was at an end, I had to break through, the wall of conditioning, that says marriage is forever, no matter what, the rules and regulations of the Catholic church I was reared by, the attitudes of people around me and last, but not least the expectations of myself, parents and ancestral line. After a lot of clearing, I gifted myself permission to follow my heart, and leave a trail, rather than follow the footsteps of others. I was in the frontline, the first to separate in my family. A lot of people stepped away and love and support for me, was only gifted by a few, who I will never forget and am eternally grateful for. I shivered and shook through the birthing process of the separated woman, but I knew I was being guided from above and my eyes remained fixed, on the star I followed.

Chapter 9

Born Again

I lived with the boys for a time in my brother's home, before I settled in Co. Kildare, to rear them into adulthood. At the time of the separation I had driven to the Phoenix Park, an area of vast parkland in Dublin and among nature and the trees, I explained the separation to them, as best I could. One of them cried a lot, but they seemed to understand on some level and at regular intervals, I would ask how they were feeling and discuss whatever presented itself. It was very important for me and vital for them, not to criticise their Father or demean him in anyway. I made a decision not to talk about my relationship or my reasons for separating to the vast majority of people around me, as I did not want people to dismiss or judge Gerry, on my behalf. The difficulty this caused was that people made assumptions and judgements about me that were untrue and unfair. However, I got over them and I hope they did too.

Around this time, I entered a development group with my soul buddies, Anne, an acupuncturist and Joan, a psychic healer. One night a week, we journeyed together, through meditation, psychic atunement, healing and acupuncture, into our own cells, lives, and each others, working with emotional patterns, conditioned attitudes and even past life experiences. Our brief was to clear the way internally for our dreams to be born and the true nature of our beings to surface. We guided each other into dark, unexplored, scary spaces, one is often afraid to explore in oneself and held a space of love and healing for each other, while guiding the transformation of whatever was uncovered. This work laid the foundation that gave me the confidence to work in the way I now do.

I will be forever grateful to Anne and Joan for their precious skills, divine guidance and support, through that vital time of healing, exploration and discovery. It was invaluable at the time and it afforded me a safe space, as I learned to put language on, all that I tuned into. It was such a relief to convert the imprints I attuned to all around me, into words and a confidence, dawning and realisation, that this was the psychic or mediumship ability I had, was awakening in me. It was a natural gift I had, one I did not understand or know how to use, but little by little, like learning a new language, I became fluent. There were days I felt stuck in past lifetime spaces and weeks I felt trapped by old attitudes and emotions that were taking time to release. With patience and time, the clearing and transformation of the physical and emotional body becomes fast and much more efficient. My dream is that in time, it will be faster than the speed of light and the true nature and flow of the river of spiritual energy and consciousness, through our emotional and physical bodies into the Earth, will be one of free flow and ease.

As I experienced an emotional collapse and breakthrough, that saw me attending Tony Hogan's clinic, I was left with a fear that it would happen again and for a long time I felt as if I was standing near the edge of a cliff, wondering would I fall over and break my neck. Slowly, over time, as with any trauma, my confidence grew and this fear disappeared altogether. It was the social stigma of falling asunder and my pride being wounded, as people might see me as weak and unable to cope, that plagued me most. I felt myself for a long time, that I was emotionally vulnerable and intensely sensitive and had to work hard to cope with who I was and this life. The expression of my work and gifts are born out of this deep sensitivity and emotional 'atunement'. So, my weakness, as I saw it for a long time, has turned out to be my greatest strength.

I had a reading on tape from Lilla Bek and she told me I was an amazing soul, because I had started half a mile behind the start line of the race, so to speak and had worked so hard, that I was now way ahead of my time. She said I had carried a huge workload into the Earth this lifetime and as I was now ahead of schedule I needed to slow down. She also told me I shared some of her gifts. I was so relieved I was doing ok, on the right track and managing to survive. No amount of praise or acknowledgement seemed to permeate my being and awaken any real sense of pride or real inner confidence. There was just a relief that someone thought I was precious and doing ok and it would take me time, to make firm and comfortable friends with my emotional and mental self. My mid to late thirties cemented this friendship and my mind, body and soul now had a good working relationship and a quiet confidence had grown in me about my gifts and abilities.

The contract I signed with myself at twenty eight was to work with the powerful energy of my soul and to use it, as far as possible to heal my body, mind and emotions. With regard to my body, a healthy diet and exercise was a vital part of my routine, but by far the biggest change I made, was to stop taking prescribed medication and to work with my body-mind/emotions-soul, if I became ill. A good example of this is a back pain I had that was so severe I could hardly walk, sit on the loo or move. I was in agony and used acupuncture, healing and other natural methods to ease the pain. After being confined to bed for weeks I went into meditation and asked what was going on emotionally and spiritually. Instantly, I was drawn to what I just knew was a past lifetime space, where I was being crucified and sacrificed. I visualised becoming a giant, entering the space, taking myself off the cross, bathing and healing myself. Afterwards I drew a picture of this time, wrote and cried and then I drew an image of myself free and healed. Within twenty four hours my back was dramatically better and I never looked back. The back relates to the spine and imprints of past lifetimes often lodge in the spine, to be released later.

When the physical body is having symptoms or is ill, it is seeking to release and heal, to make way for your soul, real self, energy and gifts to be expressed. I made a choice to work with my physical body in this way and at times it took weeks to clear what was going on, but the progress I made physically, emotionally, mentally and spiritually was worth it. I chose not to suppress my symptoms with drugs, but work with them, in as natural a way as possible. Since twenty eight years of age, I have only needed an odd tooth anaesthetic. However, the process of learning how to work in this way with myself has been frightening at times and a powerful lesson in deepening my trust and understanding of the link between the body, mind-emotions and soul. Taking responsibility for my own health, giving time for my body to heal if it was ill and expressing the emotions or patterns that were being cleared through that illness, brought up fears of serious illness such as cancer. I used these fears as an opportunity to explore what cancer was and how one could work with it, and also to express and release the fear that what happened my Mother was going to happen to me.

When I bought a new home recently and needed a medical for insurance purposes, my childhood doctor was quite amazed at how healthy I was and that I managed to live my life without drugs or medication. My dream would be that prescribed medication and painkillers would be used in cases of serious or terminal illness. Leading up to the stress and excess of this Christmas time, I was amused to see the many cleverly crafted advertisements for various headache tablets, echoing the silent reminder that we could not possibly live through Christmas without them!

My healing work continued and people were now coming to me for sessions, instead of me visiting their homes. I had become a full healing member of the N.F.S.H. and as such had the qualification necessary by earthly standards.

A tall and very beautiful young woman with four small children came to me with cancer. Let us call her Lily. A friend made an appointment for Lily, telling me she had terminal cancer with secondary cancer in her liver, asking me not to discuss the 'terminal' bit with her, as she thought she was cured. Being a raw recruit in the healing world, I agreed (a one and only time) and confined myself to discussing the underlying emotional issues related to the type of cancer she had, and how she could work with them. She fully understood what the underlying issues were and kept promising to work with them, but as often happens, she did not get around to it, perhaps because the changes she may have found it necessary to make, felt too difficult in this life. A very powerful aspect of her healing experience was that she became very well for a period, despite her very grave medical prognosis, a time that enabled her to socialise, catch up and have lots of fun with friends and family.

Alongside the touch healing, I was now doing creative visualisations with clients and Lily loved these, falling into a deeply relaxed state, remembering every word and practicing them at home. She would recite them while having invasive medical procedures, refusing medication, to the amazement of the staff. What people around her thought were ramblings and ravings, I knew to be the visual meditations I had done with her, that she recited by heart. I grew to love Lily very much and she me. Her case was so close to the bone, reminding me of my Mother.

A part of me desperately wanted her to get better, to do something for her I had not been able to do for my Mother. She patiently taught me, to honour her journey and I supported her to die with dignity, courage and peace in her heart. I was asked to tell her children she was dying. It was one of the hardest jobs I was ever asked to do. With my soul buddy Anne, we devised a story and I took the children in my arms and told them that story, to prepare them gently for their Mother's death. It felt heartbreaking.

As the time grew closer, I would drive to Lily's home and later to the hospital, often crying a lot on the journey, for my Mother, for Lily, her children and husband and for the real truth of being a healer that I was now learning. She was one of my greatest teachers and near the end she spoke to me of her fear of leaving the children and I assured her she could organise things and Mother them from the heavens. She spoke of her fears of the fires of hell and that she would go there. I held her hands, explained this was just her fear based on her religious conditioning, answered her questions and did healing and visual meditative journeys with her. She was suffering a lot now and I realised that her fear of letting go, was causing her to use the healing to hold on.

One winter evening I attended a choral sevice, during which I meditated and begged her to let go, sending her a mental message that I was letting her go. Lily died that night. For a while before she died she could see those she knew from the spirit world all around her and she said they gave her a message for me, a message that touched my heart very deeply. She said they told her I had special gifts and I was going to do precious work in the World and she was going to help me from the other side. That confirmation from spirit meant the world to me. Lily died a peaceful death and organised a wonderful childminder for her children. I was broken in by Lily and taught the basic premise of healing, to support a person on their journey, whatever that is. I felt honoured and blessed to have been chosen by her, as her midwife, as she birthed into spirit. Since then, I have supported many people on their journeys from this world to the next.

One Easter Sunday morning, I was requested by some members of a family, to visit their home and do healing on their Mam. Let us call her Primrose. She was confined to a wheelchair, hospitalised, unable to speak or move for one too many years, as a result of a severe stroke. She was trapped in her body, unable to communicate and her family knew she was sad, weary and unable to leave. As I did healing on her and guided her through a visual meditation that connected her with the light of healing and heaven, her guides and angels, her own worthiness and those she loved in spirit, the tears flowed constantly down her face. She saw the bridge in her consciousness that connected heaven and earth and I brought Primrose across that bridge during the healing session, to bathe in the love and light of spirit and family and guided her to see herself, free and well again. There were powerful emotional and spiritual energies in the room, causing my tears to flow also. Primrose was deeply grateful, connected so absolutely to me and the gift I brought and told me without speaking, but with every fibre of her being, how grateful she was. I guess I was her angel that morning. I felt honoured to take that preparatory journey with her. My absolute love of chocolate came a poor second to the wow I experienced that Easter Sunday. Primrose died peacefully shortly after.

These are just two examples of the many people I have been blessed to work with in this way, over the last twenty years. Many people have come psychically to ask for my support, just before I fall asleep, as I wake, during the night, in meditation or at quiet times. I then journey into a meditative space and gift them the light, love and healing they have asked for. I can journey quite far into the spirit world without any fear and it is true to say that in the past, I have been more comfortable with the spirit world, than the earth.

Healing has asked me to work with many people who have been bereaved, through illness, accident and suicide. A man came to me once, very distraught, as his wife had committed suicide, leaving him and the children, so shockingly and suddenly. Let us call him Jake. This very intense and painfully difficult situation, opened Jake's emotional body and he experienced intense anger, sadness, loss, betrayal, loneliness and abandonment. I supported him to honour those feelings and express them in a number of different ways. He had many questions and I would tune in for him and seek the answers, but the 'piece de resistance', was the result of a 'bereavement workshop' I facilitated, where during meditation he could, feel, smell, touch and communicate with his wife in spirit. Jake was elated. The healing journey I facilitated with him was complete and he continued with his own personal journey of spiritual discovery. Just like Jake reconnected with his partner in spirit, with time and patience, it is possible for everyone to learn the language of this type of communication. It requires a person to journey through the fog of their deepest feelings, release the way we communicate in the Earth and open their minds and hearts to new possibilities. The connection with those in spirit is the missing link in bereavement therapy.

Another example is a young woman, who we will call Kylie. Her Father made the appointment as he was afraid Kylie was going to commit suicide, as her fiancé had died. They had been partners for many years and were close to getting married. She was devastated and just wanted to die. As I worked with her through healing and emotional support, some personal information given to me from spirit soothed her and gave her the proof she needed, that he was still there and very much in love with her. It gave Kylie the strength to go on and continue with her life.

A last example of the many I could choose from is about a young man we will call Mark. Mark came to see me, after his wife had died, quite quickly from cancer. She got sick not long after they married and he cared for her lovingly and patiently, until the day she died. He was so lonely he would play their wedding video over and over, rarely leaving the house. The healing sessions we did were spent processing emotions and journeying into the spirit world, through meditation, again and again, to connect with his young wife. Eventually, he could connect so freely and easily with her that he was able to turn off the video and continue living, knowing she was guiding, loving and supporting him along the way.

I work with guides, angels, spirit friends and family of those that come to me and a loved one often steps in, to guide the healing session. It is interesting for me to observe the powerful and positive effect it has on a person and their lives, when I guide them in a meditative space to receive healing and love from someone they miss, who is in the spirit world, through visualising being stroked, receiving the rose pink light of divine love, a dove of peace or being held.

I have worked with exam students, who were experiencing severe stress, locked hands unable to write and minds gone blank. Always now, I close my eyes and journey into the 'cell memories' of that person, to see what is written and felt there and what is the root cause of the stress or given situation. Just like the memory bank in our computers, the cells of our bodies, record everything we experience and feel. Also recorded in the cells, are past lifetime events, genetic and generational patterns, wisdom gathered from past and present lifetimes, gifts and talents, dreams and ideals. In my next book, I hope to explore 'cellular memory patterns' and how to work with them. The journeying into these patterns and doing guided meditative journeys, to clear, develop and transform them, in order to give birth to ones heart, free spiritedness and life's dreams and ideals, is the essence of my gift and what I do. The evolvement to reading and understanding those patterns, in the way I now do, happened over time. Creative visual meditations evolved into personal guided meditative journeys, which I call 'Merlin moments' and give on tape to each client.

I have worked with many people who have been sexually abused, some of them in the most horrendous of ways. Numerous women have come to me, that have experienced this type of abuse, so I have decided collectively to call them Brooke and give you an example or broad outline of the type of shared experience I have had with them. Brooke was brutally and repeatedly sexually assaulted and it took great courage and bravery for her to come for healing sessions and trust me enough, to share her very painful story, that she had hidden since childhood. The first part of the healing I facilitated with her was to be compassionate, loving and available to listen to Brooke's story, to create a safe space for her to be supported and encouraged to express and release deep emotions. Such horrendous abuse causes deep pain and also opens a person to other deep pain held in the cells, needing to be released. An abused child may feel anger, hatred, intense fear, deep loss, sadness, and so forth, with her abuser, parents, society and even herself. As we moved through Brooke's emotions, we journeyed in to look at and send healing to her own attitudes, towards herself and her family and anything that would leave her vulnerable to abuse in the World. How we often find ourselves exposed to different situations in our lives, I will explore in more detail, in my next book on 'cellular memory', as it is a subject deserving intense scrutiny.

Brooke experienced layers of healing on many different levels and in time, made peace in her heart with what had happened to her and forgave (while not condoning) her abuser. She is now happy and fulfilled in her life. Brooke found the courage to use this horrendous experience, as a spiritual gateway to self development and huge evolvement on an emotional and spiritual level. I felt honoured that she trusted me and allowed me access to her innermost kingdom. I am constantly reminded that love brings about and facilitates powerful healing, the love we give ourselves; receive from spirit, the people around us, nature, animals, music and literature.

I have worked with many clients, who presented with a variety of relationship issues, some desiring to bring their relationship onto the next level, others wanting to separate, many seeking relationships and those women who are trapped in violent relationships, terrified to move or even acknowledge their pain. One such woman comes to mind. We will call her Hazel. She was a prisoner for the most part in her relationship and her home, unless her husband gave her permission to go out, for a short monitored period. This man was very violent and threatened to kill her, if she left him. If she argued or had an opinion, he would become violent. She had handed the reins of her life to this violent man and even when he said it was ok to go out, she was convinced his evil eye was trained on her. She lived in terror. On one of her 'passes' she found the courage to come to me.

I worked with Hazel over a period of time, journeying into her cells, to support her to heal the spaces, where she had lost her self esteem and self worth. This meant going back to her childhood, difficult relationships with her parents and limiting critical belief patterns about herself and changing them. I supported her to put in place legal protection in the Earth around her. Eventually Hazel left her husband, knowing she was protected spiritually and legally. Her husband did not try to murder her, as he had threatened to do numerous times. She is a happy, independent woman now. Again, I am grateful to Hazel for trusting, opening and allowing me to be her guide. Every new client challenges me and becomes my teacher. Every situation is different and there is always something new to be learned.

I support every client, to embark on a journey of falling in love with, themselves, loving, respecting, honouring and nurturing themselves, and then sharing themselves with the World and others, in ways they are comfortable with. We all naturally want to gift ourselves and our love and it would be so lovely if we chose to do this, in ways that make our hearts sing. If we look at nature as our guide and teacher – it nurtures itself first, then it shares its fruit with us. I have worked with many clients over the years, in many different ways. There are those who I have supported, to transform themselves and their lives and there are those who I have worked so hard to reach, yet feel I have not gotten there. There are the people who come for one session, acknowledge the accuracy of what I have attuned to, but choose never to return, or to work on their issues. I can only hope that they know it is possible to do so, one day, when they are ready.

Then, there is a woman I will call Nora, who came to groups I facilitated and to a few individual sessions. She was married to an abusive man and had small children. Nora turned to alcohol and she reached out for support to me and a number of other people. She eventually separated from this man, but the abuse continued. At times she seemed to be doing well and getting her life on track, but at other times she hit the bottle. She had huge lack of self esteem despite her obvious beauty and gentleness. She went to a residential care centre for alcoholism and after she was doing well or so I thought. I lost touch with her for many years, when recently, while rambling through Dublin city, I was shocked to see her as a down and out alcoholic, dirty, sitting on the pavement, very drunk and drinking. I felt broken hearted and found myself crying, that I had not been able to reach her. It was humbling and yes there was a lesson in it.

Healing is a gift given and Nora has the right to use it as she pleases, but also it is cumulative like money in the bank, which means that all the support, light, love and guidance she received is stored somewhere in her inner being, like treasures waiting to be uncovered someday, when she is ready. I placed her in the arms of her spirit guide, surrounded her with golden light, asked for her protection and let her go. I beseech heaven every now and then for favours and I tell them they owe me one, as I work hard for them. Nora, may your inner wings continue to grow and just when you are ready, may they stretch across the Universe, enabling you to claim the beauty of all that you are.

Around this time also, I began to facilitate groups and workshops and this aspect of my work continued quite intensively over the following ten years. The Vocational Education Committee ran adult education classes in the evenings and requested of me to tutor the 'Holistic Living' programme. It was a nerve wracking experience to begin with, as I had no experience with groups. But for my Father had his hand spiritually at my back, I think I would have run away. It was daunting to sit, facilitating a group, in a room filled with expectant faces, but as I loved my subject, in time my confidence grew, the fears transformed and I got a lot of positive feedback. The group work expanded to, women's study groups, meditation circles, spiritual development classes and so forth. I covered an array of subjects from relationship issues, dreams and goals, self care, death and dying, anger, forgiveness and stress management. I used lots of different techniques, some of which are, drawing, writing, words and music, and every issue culminated in a transformational meditation.

For many years, the women attending the groups would tell their husbands, they were doing yoga, as there was a lot of reaction to this type of work, in those years. It was undercover work in a way, for most of these women and I watched with great satisfaction as they grew, expanded and developed, awakening to the full potential and knowingness, of their individuality and uniqueness. I loved this group work and it added a new and different dimension to what I did.

The group session that seemed to excite people most, was the result of an effort on my part, to bring healing to those who had been bereaved, which was almost everyone, in every group. I would guide them on a meditative journey into the spirit world, where they would meet their loved ones, and receive messages, love or healing in some form or other. I would also tune in for them at times, via a photograph they would bring of their loved one and gift them the messages I received. I was often a bit tentative about the messages I received from spirit, not fully trusting my ability to interpret them correctly or afraid I would get it wrong. Regularly, I received notes and cards, telling me to trust my ability and drop everything else to concentrate on this communication with spirit. How right they were re my gift, as the foundation of my work now is tuning in to spirit and the cell memories of an individual. These women greatly encouraged and supported my gifts and I focused on guiding them into the deepest meditative spaces of healing and transformation.

The group work I facilitated expanded into full day and

weekend workshops and I also explored and facilitated a number of 'stress management' training days, in the business world. The corporate stress management days, were attended mainly by men and while the feedback was very positive, these men who I interviewed individually admitted their need for regular and ongoing stress management workshops, but they were totally reluctant to admit this to management, in case it was interpreted as 'you cant hack it', or you wont get promotion.

How sad that society's attitudes are so rigid and it is not surprising that men of our era, experience a lot of heart problems. We need to embrace the emotional expression, development and growth of men in our World and to support them to embrace this in themselves. Emotions are not the domain of women alone. Beginning with our children, we can encourage them to share their feelings and their tears and to know it is ok to feel. We do not necessarily need to give them the answers but rather create a loving and compassionate space, where they can express and be heard. As we empty from within, the answers grow inside us. With younger children, expression through art and movement works very well, as does healing and subliminal messages when they are sleeping, much like I did with Kenn, when he had warts.

One little girl I treated, was very anxious and frightened of leaving her home and going to school. Her parents had separated and she had no language to process her questions, fears and feelings. We drew a lot together, but she would only use the colour black (as black hides everything), hiding herself from the World. When I suggested using colour, she cried hysterically, terrified to express who she was, so during healing and guided meditation I introduced colour in her minds eye and how safe it was to express and be who she was. Before long, we had colour everywhere. She regained her confidence, went back to school and never looked back.

Children are like sponges, absorbing everything and they are more than capable of processing things, once we find a language of expression that suits their individual needs. It is important that we do not assume they have not noticed, or that there is no way to language their experiences. They are perhaps more open than we are to learning and growing, through the many different formats of language that are presented to them. Let us not underestimate the power of our children and how working with them now, can vastly change their individual universe and the future of our planet.

Another little girl had experienced the death of a sibling. She was wetting her bed, having nightmares, unable to sleep properly. I went to visit her home late at night, to do healing on her and I sent her mental messages as she slept, reconnecting her with her brother. Healing came very quickly and she was soothed and comforted, all of her symptoms of pain and trauma disappearing, enabling her to sleep peacefully again. My experience is that healing works quite rapidly for children. They are open, trusting and willing to drink the magical healing colours and energies of the universe.

Sometimes as adults, we encase our hearts and minds in mistrust, doubt and wariness and a sense of – prove it to me and I will step in. How have we travelled so far away from our sense of spirit and the energy of divine love? Our pathway to healing and balance in our society has to be one that brings us back in touch with spirit and the essence of the heart. The further away we go, the harder we become and the violent crime and war in our society spreads. It is a cry for help and a need to educate our leaders, governments, adults and children alike in the arenas of emotional and spiritual development, so we step back into the awareness of spirit and the balancing energy of divine healing love. I do believe love is the greatest healer of all. We must contract to express and heal our own hearts and that healing is then automatically gifted on to those around us and to our Universe.

An otherworldly happening occurred during tea/coffee break, after a meditation evening I was facilitating to celebrate Easter. I was in a room chatting and having tea with participants, when an old lady, dressed in tweeds, who seemed very troubled, stood at the door, asking could she speak to me. I said I would be with her in a moment, puzzled as I had not observed her in the group. She headed into the meditation room and after a few moments I followed her. She had disappeared into thin air. No-one had seen her leave. Niamh, who had looked after the registration of those that attended, said there was no one answering that description in the group. One astute participant, who had observed this woman, said she was puzzled, as the woman seemed to have disappeared without a trace. I came to know she was from spirit, so I sent her healing for a while. There were no return visits.

Another visit from spirit happened after Sean, the father of one of my soul buddies died. I had worked with Sean when he was ill with cancer and during those sessions, he vividly described seeing (in meditation) a Tibetan guide, again and again. Just before Sean died, I joined my friend Joan and her family to do healing on him, to ease his birth into spirit. After the healing, this small Tibetan man, entered the room, stood at the end of the bed, joined his hands and bowed in Sean and Nancy (his wife's) direction. He never uttered a word, just turned and left the room. We felt he was Sean's guide as no-one had seen him before or since and it would not be usual to have a Tibetan man, unable to speak the English language, wandering through a hospice in Dublin. He entered the room very shortly before Sean died. He came to accompany Sean along the pathway into the spirit World, just as he had silently supported him through every moment of his life, and also to bring some magical healing love to Sean's wife and family.

Close to my mid thirties, a soulmate came into my life. For some time I had been asking heaven for a soulmate as I was lonely emotionally and spiritually and had felt this way for as long as I could remember. I desired a soulmate, who was comfortable with my deep sensitivity, emotions and spiritual ideals. This had to be someone I could share all of me with. It was a luxury I had never experienced before, but something I ached for. I did not immediately recognise this person as my soulmate, as they arrived in a most unexpected guise. The sharing of this story requires a book all to itself, one I will write in the future. Suffice to say, that lonely space within me, was filled.

Chapter 10

Letting Go

As well as doing my healing work and facilitating groups, I was rearing Kenn and Davin, whose schedule I worked around and they also facilitated me, by being quiet at certain times, as I saw individual clients, in a healing room, in my own home. I became very tired in my late thirties and early forties, as I was being a mother to the boys, facilitating groups at least three nights a week and doing individual healing work. My first contract had been with the boys and my first breath of responsibility was to them, so I decided to cut back hugely on group work, so I could recharge.

Kenn and Davin settled down in Leixlip, attending a co-ed community college nearby. As they reached the stage of the older teen, their friends would congregate in our home, have a few drinks, and regale me with funny antics and stories and head to the local disco, often waking me up, like giggling girls, in the wee hours of the morning.

I loved the house being filled with their friendship, fun, laughter, youth and carefree attitudes. It was like having an extended family.

I always tried to keep an open forum for communication and expression with the boys. Kenn spilled everything out (even those things you might not have wanted all the details of)! And he followed me around, incessantly, asking questions, until he was about sixteen. I, on the other hand, probably drove Davin mad, prodding, poking and asking questions, when he seemed quiet or down. He was naturally a quiet child, who pondered a lot on things internally. If he really has something he needs to express now, it usually spills out. Maybe the prodding and poking served its purpose.

I had such a close relationship with the boys that I could never envisage a time, when they and all their friends, would not be living with us. The time was fast approaching, when I would have to let them go. I had always encouraged independence in them, as I was very independent myself and even though I was deeply committed to my healing work, soulmate, family, friendships, sport and hobbies, nothing prepared me for the level of loss I experienced when they left. One night, about a year, before they left, I was ill and woke up in the middle of the night, vividly aware that the time was coming, and I howled like a wolf that was losing her cubs. I wanted them to grow up and have every opportunity to follow their stars and live out their dreams, but I did not want to lose them and that is what I was most afraid of. There was no parent or any other person I knew around me, that would teach me about these things. Maybe every Mother feels this. I did not know. I loved being a Mother and losing that identity, on a daily basis, was a whole new learning experience. Through my tears, I saw glimpses of light relief. I would not have to make dinner, choose what they would eat or have to clean up, but it was small comfort when compared with what I was about to lose.

Money has always been a challenge and while Gerry gave me maintenance for the boys, every penny I earned and a couple of re-mortgages went towards our living expenses. My work ebbed and flowed like the tides, so the standard of my income was irregular, but I worked around it, as I did not want to give up my beloved healing, which was, after all, like a vocation to me, not just a job. It was the breath of who I was and how I lived, expressed, thought and processed my life. To this day, what I teach, how I work, is who I am and how I live my life. There is no separation between me and what I do. We are one.

In 1999, my 'soulmate' became very ill and as I had received huge support and sharing, on a personal level and with rearing the boys, (something I will always be extremely grateful for), this was a huge blow to me. I found myself alone again and struggling to keep my head above water emotionally and financially, as everything seemed to be collapsing all around me. Just under a year later, Davin left school and was offered a place, in a prestigious furniture design college, some six hours drive away. He was eighteen years old. Kenn was twenty and had done some stock market training. His interest at that time was finance but he was still looking for his niche. They both left home within a month of each other. Davin went to study and live deep in rugged beautiful Connemara, among the many lakes and mountains of the west of Ireland. He would come home every two to three months and I travelled to see him a number of times. Kenn moved to work and live in Waterford, for my brother, some three and a half hours drive away. He came home more often at the weekends.

Essentially, my beloved boys were gone. They had flown the nest. It was hard to breathe just for me. Scatter, Kenn's cat of thirteen years, who I had reared with the boys, had died a few years previously. Now Jesse, my 'soulmates' dog and my faithful pal, who had lived with us for ten years, was losing his hearing and howling, from his frightening new and silent world. I guess he reflected me in some way. The house was an empty nest, except for me and Jesse. I felt I had lost everyone all over again, my 'soulmate', the boys, their friends, Scatter and now Jesse was howling for release, a release plea I did not want to hear, until one day I looked out the window and into Jesse's eyes and I saw my Father staring back at me, telling me Jesse had to come to him. It was his time. He would look after him. In that moment, my Father passed me so much information, that I could see Jesse running free, in the green fields of spirit. I howled yet again, but began preparing to let Jesse go. I wrote, cried, had some healing and homeopathy and retreated into meditation, where I received strength, to begin again.

I had to release the shell of my old world, in order to be reborn and I felt very raw and vulnerable for some time, but my training in processing and meditation guided me through. In a way, I was angry with the World for taking my boys away so young, when all my friends still had their children at home, but being Pisceans like me, they were driven by their own ideals. They had my blessing. I just missed them so badly, it hurt in every cell of my being and I felt abandoned in this big home, all on my own. I knew there was a nugget of wisdom and learning in this situation, so I kept breathing, walking, saying mantras, meditating, learning and being carried by spirit and those that loved me. I also felt like a wimpy Mother for feeling this way, but perhaps every Mother feels like this. I had to honour how I felt. Kenn moved back from Waterford to work in Dublin and moved in with his girlfriend Celine and her daughter Richelle. Davin loved his own space and was not planning on living at home again. So, I had some decisions to make.

I began to dream again, for me and in 2002, my 'soulmate' had recovered and we made a decision to take six months off work, to travel to U.S.A. and Australia. Selling everything, and paying off any outstanding debts, saw us banking a large deposit for a new home in the future and funding this trip, I had always wanted to take. Letting everything go was scary, but I needed to redefine me and my life. I had worked long and hard for this space I was about to gift to myself and share with my 'soulmate'. I struggled with my invisible duties as a Mother. Mothers were not supposed to do this sort of thing. They stayed at home and held the space, should their children every want to come home. It did not look like my two would be doing that. Kenn and Celine were saving for a house and Davin was studying away for this third year. I, on the other hand, had put my children first all of my life, except for the one half hearted time, when I had considered going to the United States to work, as I was very worried and concerned, about the state of my finances and making a consistent living, and how I would survive financially in the World, as an older person. It was time to put me first and for the first time in my adult life, I was going to do something completely and entirely for me. It was like claiming my heart and soul completely.

I had given everything I could possibly find, within my heart and soul, as a Mother and the only regret I really have, is that prior to going to Tony Hogan, when the kids were very little, I gave them what was considered 'a slap' with my hand, at times, when they were very challenging. As I grew and developed and society evolved, I learnt new ways of guiding, their growth and development, ways that did not include any physical punishment, no matter how mild. It is interesting to note the evolutionary process of disciplining ones children. My Mother told stories of my Grandfather taking off his belt and walloping them with the buckled side. She on the other hand used a softer leather strap. I used my hand when the boys were very young at times and then stopped altogether, so somehow that stopping was the end of an era traditionally. So I apologise to the boys for not knowing better, from the very beginning.

I had a lot of fun times with my young sons. We played a lot together. I read stories to them each night before they went to sleep and I sang to them in the car. They felt a little like my arms and legs. Gerry and I brought them to the Burren in Co. Clare and Cape Clear island in West Cork, as I wanted them to inhale their roots and the energy, power and wisdom of their grandparents and ancestors and I pray that I have gifted them the breath of the ocean, so they may expand and grow into the freedom of being individual, unique, free spirited and all that they can be. It is the greatest gift that I can think of giving them and they of course had my love in abundance and always will. However, I was not a pushover and there were clear and definite boundaries. Bedtime was at seven and there was no negotiation, unless you were ill or there was a celebration, holiday or party. Apart from the odd moments of frustration about being on call twenty four seven, Mothering was a joy for me and it gave me confidence and a clear identity in the Earth.

I was going to miss the boys a lot, but they were out living their lives and I needed to find the courage and confidence, to live mine. I will be forever grateful to them for choosing me as their Mother and for the adventure of growing up, we shared together.

Nowadays, they are busy with their lives. I don't see them nearly often enough. We talk on the phone from time to time and meet up when possible. I still miss them a lot sometimes, but I am learning to live for me, more and more each day. No-one taught me how to be a Mother with adult children, as my Mother died, when I was entering adulthood. I had no role model, but I am feeling my way instinctively, step by step. We have not fully established an adult relationship yet, but I am sure it is on the way. They are both doing well in their respective journeys and I am proud of them. May they experience the breath of freedom and fulfilment, as their dreams and wishes, are born into the earth.

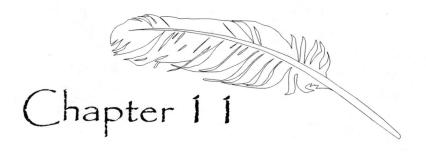

Chapter 11

The Great Adventure

The great adventure began in October 2002, as I had arrived at the 'fully grown up' age of forty six. I felt great excitement prior to the trip and though it was emotionally shaky just before departure, somewhere deep inside, I knew this trip was right for me. Our first port of call was Staten Island, New York and I was filled with excitement as we approached the airport and watched the United States of America open itself to us. It was a first for me, as my only other landing in the U.S. had been as a transit passenger, en route to the Bahamas.

It was crisp and cold in New York and the memory of 9/11 still hung in the air. We took a ferry to Staten Island and paid an emotional salute to the 'Statue of Liberty', as we sailed by. She represented the guardian of this trip. It was the first time as an adult that I felt completely free, free of the responsibilities of rearing a family, paying a mortgage, running a home and working to make ends meet. I had a peculiar feeling of guilt for some time. I should be working, living a 'normal' life and earning a living. Also I felt a bit insecure, as if a familiar blanket had been whipped away, as there were no friends or family here, no familiar home space and no one we knew. What if anything happened? I comforted myself with the knowing that they were only a plane ride away and I concentrated on a meditation, where I saw myself put my roots deep down in the soil of this country that nurtured and held me at this time.

Our guesthouse was nestled at the edge of the ocean, looking across the bay at the magic of the New York skyline. Sitting on the beach, bathed in autumn sunshine, the ocean lapping gently at my feet, I watched the giant ships sailing into New York harbour, pondered on the changed city skyline and the horrendous shock and brutality of 9/11 and the giant scar it left, that was in the process of healing.

I thought of the many generations of Irish people who had come before me, landing on Ellis Island en route to their new homes, forced to leave Ireland because of famine and poverty. I thought of my aunt and uncle who had come to live here as a young married couple. And, I felt lucky, blessed, to be sitting on this beach, experiencing those moments of freedom, tears, pondering, adventure and having the opportunity to taste and digest the spirit of New York. During our nine days here, we visited Ellis Island, the first port of call for immigrants to the United States, the site of 9/11, the Guggenheim, Central Park and much more.

Before long and with a promise to return, we flew to Florida and took a greyhound bus, across the many bridges, that spanned for countless miles across the sea, to Key West, the southernmost island in the United States. Key West has a Cuban influence, heat in the mid thirties, very pretty houses and the most amazing trunk formations on the giant Jackaranda trees. We booked in to a private room in a local hostel and went in search of, what turned out to be, a very pretty harbour. Our reason for coming to Key West was to swim with wild bottlenose dolphins in warm waters. It was an expensive luxury we were so looking forward to.

Our previous experience swimming with dolphins in the wild had been with 'Fungi', the solitary world renowned Dingle dolphin, in southern Ireland. My first experience with 'Fungi' happened one day as I stood at the end of a pier looking out to sea. He vaulted directly up out of the water and looked into my eyes. I was overcome with a mix of powerful emotions, joy, love, power, freedom and from that moment on I was hooked. Sometime later, in mid winter and clad in rubber from head to toe, my brother took us out in a boat and as 'Fungi' danced around us, wanting to play, I tentatively got into the freezing deep Dingle waters. It had begun to snow and as it was my first time in a wetsuit and fins and being confronted by a giant enormous male bottlenose dolphin, I freaked and screamed at my brother to get me out of the water. I took it more gently after that, getting in and out of the water from the beach, during the summer months, snorkelling with 'Fungi' at every opportunity.

We spent ten days in Key West, the life of a butterfly and many of these days were spent drifting around in a beautiful catamaran, watching a pod of dolphins, riding the bow wave, dancing, playing and vaulting out of the water with most daring and amazing acrobatic displays. These dolphins were always on the move, so the opportunities we had to snorkel, involved leaping from the boat and snorkelling along fast behind them. While I am a good swimmer and well able to snorkel, I am wary in the ocean and need time to adjust, so most often in the water, the dolphins were gone on ahead of me, except for the day one vaulted right over my head. Later, in Australia, I was to have the 'wow' dolphin experience in the water. Those days on the water with the dolphins were healing, magical and soothing for the soul. It was a little like a drug. There was a feeling of being on a high and never wanting to leave.

Dolphins are often called the 'angels of the sea' and they definitely have a very positive healing effect on human beings. Of course, they are wild animals and above all else, one needs to respect their space, but they are also gentle giants that seem to radiate, a soothing, loving and fun vibration. I have swum among pods in different oceans and never once did I feel threatened. Yes, there is an adjustment period of learning to trust, that you are safe, with these giant creatures. The key seems to be, to allow the dolphins come to you and then to swim or snorkel gently alongside them, until they choose to leave. There were also many beautiful shops, galleries and restaurants in Key West. Before long, it was time to leave and I watched the beautiful colours of the rising sun, bathe the Florida keys, as we made our way back to the Airport.

Our next port of call was Niagara Falls in Canada. We left Key West early one morning, in 35 degrees C of heat and arrived shivering, late at night in Toronto at minus 2 degrees C. Another long bus ride in the early hours of the morning to Niagara left us exhausted, disorientated and freezing. It was a temperature shock as well as a culture shock. We travelled from the calm beauty of the crystal clear waters around Key West to the brash, loud, commercialised atmosphere of Niagara Falls. The magical vista of the falls, the loud roar of its song and the thunderous trip beneath the falls, were all spectacular and exciting in themselves. However, apart from the falls and a pretty pink pair of Nike runners, 'out of there', we could not wait to get.

We flew next to San Francisco, picked up our hired car at the airport, spent a night in San Fran and journeyed the following day to 'Yosemite National Park'. It was my 'soulmate', who wanted to go to Yosemite, so I just tagged along, knowing nothing whatever about the area, other than it was a nature reserve and as I love nature that was fine with me. I was definitely not prepared for what happened next.

We stayed in private facilities in a most beautiful hostel, owned by an Irish woman, nestled among giant pine trees, that was situated some twenty minutes drive from Yosemite. The following day we headed to the Park and from the moment we drove through the entrance, deep powerful emotions began to stir in me. Apart from the majestic beauty of the high mountains, the tinkle of the flowing river, the roar of the waterfall, the exquisite stellar blue jays, and the giant sequoia trees, there was something else here, that moved my soul, beyond anything I had ever experienced before. I became aware of an ancient Indian presence everywhere. Every part of my body had a heightened awareness. As we drove in, I could 'see' the spiritual silhouettes of the Indians, astride their horses, on the mountain ridges. I could 'see' clearly, the prints on their Indian blankets, which I later saw examples of in the Yosemite Indian culture museum. I could 'hear' them speaking to me. It was like being in two worlds at the same time. We parked in the centre and headed towards the reconstruction of the Indian village.

As we approached, the name of the tribe 'Ahwahneechee' was written and I was overcome with such emotion, when I saw this name I could not even pronounce. As I cried tears of recognition, I knew beyond shadow of a doubt that this had been my tribe, and I had lived here in the past. I was so overcome, that I found it difficult to walk into the village. This was the most psychic experience I had ever had. I always knew I had an Indian guide and now he was bringing me home, to a space within myself and to an ancient homeland of mine, to awaken to all the wisdom I had gathered there in the past and to my deepest dreams.

While in Yosemite I was in heaven, in my element and almost constantly in an altered ecstatic state of consciousness. During a meditative state I entered there, the guides told me I had been a 'medicine woman' during my lifetime here and that they (the guides) called me 'White Feather'. I cried a lot during this meditation, but most especially when I heard 'my name', as I have always loved swans and been drawn to white feathers. There was no question or doubt about anything I was hearing. I was 100% sure that what I was hearing was accurate.

Later, an Australian visionary artist, who knew absolutely nothing about me, drew a picture of me as an ancient Indian medicine woman and she said 'they' would not let her finish the picture, until she drew in the white feather. She explained it was a picture of me from a past life. This was a huge confirmation, of all that I had tuned into and felt during my time in Yosemite. The difficulty was that I did not want to leave and I even pondered on spending a year there. I began to feel anxious and sad as the time approached. The night before we left, I dreamt of the many generations that had gone before and the passage of time and I was clearly told it was my time to leave, now that I had gathered what I needed from my ancient home place. This did not stop me grieving for some time after. I missed them, the feeling of the tribe surrounding me, their scent, their sound, their silhouettes, and the huge spiritual connection I felt with the place and the raw natural beauty of this space and how it spoke to me and wrapped itself around me. As we left, I saw the Indians astride their horses, waving goodbye from the ridges of the mountain tops, it felt very emotional.

I guess we needed some rest after this powerful experience and though we wanted to explore San Francisco, our accommodation did not work out and we found ourselves taking refuge in Santa Barbara, for the remainder of our stay in the United States. It was more low key and restful here. We walked on the beach on Thanksgiving Day, alongside Americans who had come in their giant 'Winnebago's' for the holiday weekend. We took a most exciting trip, hoping to see the giant blue whales, but instead we saw 2 beautiful Orcas with their baby, some stinky minky whales and over five hundred common dolphins, who rode the bow wave, danced around the boat, somersaulting and journeying with us, guiding our trip, like the sea angels that they are. It was a most magical trip and our heartfelt thanks goes out, to that giant pod of dolphins, who awakened such joy and delight in all of us that day. We visited beautiful museums and spent a day at 'universal studios', flying through the air with E.T. and exploring the real life film sets.

Before long, it was time to go. Just before we left, I dreamt vividly of an orange butterfly with one wing stretched out, opened wide. The other wing was yet to open. Orange is the colour of nurturing and one wing of our trip was complete and we had been hugely nurtured by it. It was time to say goodbye to the United States, thank it for all it had gifted us and promise to come back and taste more of its delights in the future. We flew from Los Angeles to Perth, Australia stopping in Melbourne for an hour on route. It was a horrendous journey. With my six foot freakishly long legs, very tight seating arrangements on the plane, the passenger in front virtually resting on my lap throughout the flight along with my inability to sleep, it proved to be the longest flight I had ever undertaken and a panic and discomfort rose in me.

On arrival in Perth, my ankles resembled balloons and I felt disorientated and exhausted, not knowing quite where I was. A good cry was called for and all the confusion and exhaustion from a little too much travel washed out of me. A deep sleep followed and I awoke refreshed and ready to go again. Perth was sleepy and slow by comparison to L.A. or San Francisco. The pace was just perfect. We drove to Bunbury, yet again in pursuit of wild dolphins, booked into our Motel and headed to the dolphin discovery centre. The vast majority of our trip I had booked via the internet, before our departure.

Perth was warm and welcoming and we spent most of our time on dolphin trips or eating delicious vegetarian food. There is nowhere quite like Australia for divine vegetarian food. It was my first time to visit Perth but my second time down under.

There was a resident pod of bottlenose dolphins in the bay at Bunbury. The boat would bring us to their homestead and clad in wetsuits, fins and snorkels we would get into the water and wait for them. You could hear their clicking like a symphony all around you, before you could see them and then these gentle giants would look up at you from beneath or glide slowly past you. Thinking I was in a world of my own and totally unaware of anyone around me, as I looked down into the watery home of the dolphins, I developed the habit of talking to them through my snorkel and of course they would respond! One day as I was feeding this human/dolphin love affair, a handsome suitor swam by my side and I kept telling him how beautiful he was and how much I loved him and we swam side by side for some time, at a perfect pace, looking into each others eyes, whispering sweet nothings in each others ears, until we came close to the shore and he had to turn away as he could not risk being beached!!!!! I took my head out of the water, shouting with delight, only to find I was on my own in the water and some distance away all the other people who had been snorkelling, were on the boat hysterical with laughter, as they had eavesdropped on my love chatter with my suitor. Sound carries great distances at sea! Of course they had not heard the dolphins reply. That was for my ears only. Jealous I would say. I never did live that down until I left Bunbury of course. The wow factor was huge.

Hopefully the opportunity will present itself, at some stage, to spend six months or a year exploring the majesty and wonder of whales and dolphins in the wild.

We flew to Melbourne next, arriving just before Christmas and luckily had the facility of living with my brother Barry and his family. A gift from Barry saw us attending the vast open air concert, 'Carols by Candlelight' organised by Quantas on Christmas Eve. It was a magical vista of thousands of flickering lights, a balmy evening and a host of musical stars, among them Hayley Westenra, who had just been discovered and was about to break into the international arena. Her voice among other superb voices was one of pure gold. The evening was a real treat, one I will never forget. We explored Melbourne and the greater Victoria area over the next eleven weeks, enjoying the many facilities that are not available to us in Ireland, like the Australian open tennis grand slam, the Grand Prix, the huge footie stadiums and of course the sunshine. Between us, we had a vast array of family here, so much of our time was spent socialising and enjoying the pleasures of family down under. We were spoiled by these wonderful people in a hundred different ways.

Psychic fairs are an everyday occurrence in Australia and I was captivated by the psychic visionary artists, who drew imprints of people's spiritual guides, angels, loved ones from the spirit world or past life time images. We were so taken by this work that we attended a workshop and visionary art classes two mornings a week, for the remainder of our stay. Our medium was chalk pastels and with the expert guidance of Lyn, our visionary art tutor, we began with a quick squiggle that somehow contained hidden images that we began to seek and see and Lyn taught us how to tease out these images, giving them a solid imprint on paper. For me, it was like going into a meditation space. I was quite sure that these images were creative messages that were coming from my own deepest soul and also those in the spirit world.

The picture I had most difficulty with, was one that

contained many alien faces. I wanted to tear it up, hide it, start again, get rid of it, do anything but complete it. However, the ever patient Lyn worked with me, until I found a way to complete this artistic journey. It took two days and during this time I knew these faces were me, the alien, sensitive, different me that I wanted to hide, get rid of and protect. When I saw an image of my guide appearing in the picture and as it became a solid imprint I felt safe and all was ok. This picture also contained many white feathers and Celtic spirals. It was of course my future expression, unfolding on paper and my fear of being exposed, psychic, sensitive and different and anything that might mean I would be burnt at the stake, or hung, drawn and quartered. Somehow my guide brought healing, protection and guidance that would light the way and protect me every step of the journey. Each drawing seemed to contain a message, a healing gift, the release of an old fear and what was needed to heal that fear. It often took some time for the message to become clear to me, as I would be caught in a swirl of emotions that were seeking to imprint themselves on paper. These pictures were fascinating journeys and a very different way of working with ones soul, a way I would like to explore more deeply in the future.

The picture I loved most of all, was an image of the head of a bald beautiful being that appeared to be both male and female, with a wide open third eye, in its forehead. This picture felt as if there was nothing hidden, just an honest openness and the divine and powerful wisdom of the soul flowing through.

Davin was twenty one in late February of that year and his gift was going to be a trip to join me for the Grand Prix in Melbourne, as he is an avid fan. However, college commitments meant he could not travel, so we cut our trip a little short to surprise him on the night of his big birthday party. After recovering from the shock, he said it was the best gift he could have gotten.

It was difficult to leave the love, sunlight and easy pace of down under, despite having missed the boys, family and friends at varying intervals. It had been a life altering trip in so many ways for me. For the most part I had felt a sense of lightness or freedom, of just being in the world for me, having to take care of just me, the release of the burden of paying a mortgage and the many bills that accompany our modern way of being and the intensity and focus that accompanies having to get things done in the ordinary everyday world. My soul could breathe, relax, meander and some part of me had cemented a knowing, that anything we dreamt of was possible.

This trip had set me free in some way to pursue the next part of the journey, as an individual. I had broken with tradition in so many ways, by setting sail in the first place, and I had reconnected with a deep spiritual longing to express all that I was in the Earth. A lot of remembering had happened within me spiritually, a remembering of my gifts, talents, dreams and past.

Chapter 12

Back To The Beginning

Some five and a half months after leaving Ireland, we returned renewed, reborn, homeless and wondering how on earth we were going to return to reality. After the initial excitement of Davin's birthday party and catching up with family and friends, there was a feeling of being confused and lost, who was I and where did I belong now? My sister Marian lovingly provided a haven of rest and while there, I felt a huge pull to go and live by the ocean, in the Galway of my birth. I had been born in Galway, but my home, as a small child, had been situated directly across the bay in Co. Clare. It took a lot of persuasion, to talk my 'soulmate' into accompanying me, but a lovely cottage became available to rent, amid the wild beauty of Connemara, with a view across the bay to the hills of Clare, the Aran Islands and the Burren of my childhood. Again, this was a journey I needed to undertake and though I have always had a longing to live by the ocean, ever since

I left as a child I guess, I knew this would be temporary somehow.

Over the next eighteen months, spent in Galway, life held many beautiful moments and many challenging ones. Making a living became a priority and as my existing clients had all been based in the east side of the country, I found myself undertaking exhausting journeys to Dublin twice or three times a month. Mary, our precious friend, shared her home openly and lovingly with us, when we visited the east. Also, I began to advertise in the Galway area and clients came for sessions to my home space.

There were many beautiful moments spent walking by the ocean, swimming and snorkelling with Dusty the wild dolphin now resident across the bay, meditating on the rocks, entertaining family and friends in the cottage and then there were many lonely isolated moments and weeks when I was home alone, knowing absolutely no one in the area. I felt utterly abandoned and alone at these times and I came to realise, as this was the place of my birth, that I had come to fully clear and heal old emotions and patterns that had re-enacted themselves, when I was born. I had felt abandoned at birth and in this lifetime I had to learn how not to abandon myself. My brief was to honour, love and nurture myself fully, giving myself permission to express all my emotions, fears, dreams, wisdom and all that I was. I guess I was going back to pull out the roots of old fears and attitudes I had spent a lot of time working with, over the years. I wrote, drew, cried, walked, said mantras and took many meditative journeys back to my birth, to heal the child who felt imperfect, unworthy and very different.

What I had gathered and learnt in my life and on my trip around the World I was now taking back to the very roots of my being, in this lifetime, to the space of my birth. It was a very intense time of clearing that last piece of all I had been working with, so I could write this book and finally give myself permission, to express my voice loudly and clearly in the Earth. The healing work like the ocean came in waves and in the interim periods, life was calm and peaceful.

Early in 2004, my aunt Eileen, from Co. Clare, just across the bay, was travelling the last few months of her earthly journey. With great precision and focus, she organised her business and personal affairs, to hand to her family, to those that would continue to carry the flame. A brilliant business woman, she was leaving the Earth in her early sixties. She was a huge part of my childhood, my Mother's youngest sister and while I was a little afraid of her directness as a child and her ability 'not to put a tooth in it', as an adult, I always felt her home was a haven of welcome and a cup of tea. Shortly before her death I travelled with my sister Marian to see her and I had a one off very unusual and scary experience. It was night time and the family were chatting in the television room.

Suddenly I found myself alone in the room with Eileen. Our eyes locked and there was a frozen feeling, like a paralysis. It appeared to me at the time, that Eileen or I could not move or speak and I realised later that I lost complete consciousness of my body, a little like entering an altered state. When I came to, I moved my hand between our eyes to break the connection and I knew something very strange had happened. That action of my hand enabled us both to speak again and I realised very quickly, that my kidneys had released (in short, I wet myself).

I am super conscious of everything that happens in my body, so this was scary and had never happened before or since, in my life. I had contracted somehow to leave my body and journey with Eileen to the spirit world, if only for a moment, to pave the way, to soothe her fears, to comfort her, to show her the easy pathway to the other side, to guide her home. And in that moment, a huge fear I had experienced in childhood, of being so different and never being 'normal' enough, to fit into this World, was released. Our fears leave our bodies, through the kidneys and bladder. I journey to and from the spirit world in a conscious meditative state, regularly, but leaving my body in this way, something I would never consciously choose, was a gift to a woman who loved and nurtured me as a child. And with her 'no nonsense' approach to life, it was as if Eileen said, its time to let go that fear now and get on with it.

When I was about eight years of age, my grandmother (mam-a-mac), Eileen's mother died and I was sent to live with Eileen and my Grandfather, for a short period of time, over the Christmas season, to bring the lightness and joy of a child I guess. I shared a bedroom with Eileen and watched with fascination as she prepared for an evening out with her friends. Her red patent shoes shone with a dazzling brilliance that only a massage with 'Vaseline' could produce. Her make-up applied with precision and the 'piece de resistance' the beauty spot, applied with a dark brown pencil and last but not least, the hair piled high and backcombed within an inch of its life!

That Christmas after my Grandmothers death was a magical time for me. Santa called to visit on Christmas Eve, with a sack filled with toys, on his back, all for me, while the neighbours gathered to watch, my wide eyed wonder and excitement, at the magic of it all. So, thank you Santa Eileen for a magical memory of a most precious Christmas.

A week or so after Christmas, Eileen and I woke in the middle of the night, heard someone walking past our bedroom window, opening the window of the bedroom next to us, climbing in through the window and stepping into the room. Eileen jumped up and bolted the gold coloured lock on our bedroom door. That was my Uncle Johns (unoccupied) bedroom and as he was away working at sea, as a radio officer, he was not permitted leave, to attend his mother's funeral. I felt my grandmother came to visit his room for one last time that night, before settling in her heavenly home. Though I asked Eileen many times about what we heard that night, she always denied hearing anything, but I knew what I heard. She was somewhat psychic I guess but perhaps frightened of it.

She told me of a clear experience or visitation she had with her father after his death and how it frightened her. Only someone psychic could have taken that journey with me, as happened when I visited, shortly before she died. It was my last time to see her and she kissed my hand and looked deeply into my eyes, before I left. I cried a lot on my return to my home in Galway – a goodbye to Eileen and another part of my childhood. I continued to send healing to Eileen and I journeyed with her, through meditation, into the spirit world, many times, when she was close to death. I came back from these journeys with splitting headaches. Somehow I wanted to carry her there, so it would be gentle and easy for her. I cried a lot as she was dying, for her, my Mother and Father and to facilitate the release of my old contract of childhood, a release that would enable me to feel free enough to write this book. The headaches disappeared the day Eileen died in April 2004.

Some four weeks later, while standing at the sink, of our rented cottage in Connemara, looking across the sea at the hills of Clare, the phone rang. It was my brother Eanna, delivering the shocking news that my Uncle John, Eileen's brother, who lived in the Burren, Co. Clare, in what was my grandparent's home, had experienced a major heart attack and was very ill in a Galway hospital.

As I put the phone down, something erupted inside me and I experienced the most intense shock and pain. I rocked, cried, shook, howled with grief and pain. This could not be happening to John, to us all. Eileen had just died. As I howled, the pain in my head became so intense; I feared I would have a brain haemorrhage. My very loving and loyal 'soulmate' helped me through this space. John and I shared the same date of birth (9th March) and it was at Eileen's funeral, that I became aware of how bonded and connected we were on some level and I vowed to spend more time visiting and getting to know him better, as an adult. So, I felt cheated, and my own reaction to that call from my brother stunned me.

Where were these intense feelings coming from? I guess I was releasing many things, the deep pain locked inside me, from childhood, when we moved from these shores to the east coast and left my grandparents and family behind, the end of our ancestral home in the Burren and the link to all those I had grown up with, John and not enough time spent with him, remnants of grief for my parents, and so forth. Later, I realised John and I also shared a birth number (33), which gives an indication of ones spiritual focus or pathway through life.

I have learned a lot about death and rebirth, grief and bereavement, through personal experience and the work I have done with clients, over many years. I can relate and communicate very easily with the spirit world, stepping in and out at will. In fact, the healing and support I have been gifted for myself and others, from the spirit world, has been vast. At the most intense and challenging moments of my life, I have been carried by my guides and spirit family and for this I am deeply grateful. However, we are human emotional beings and despite our awareness and understanding, the loss and letting go of loved ones from the Earth, can be hard and painful.

John, lived on the shores of the Burren, where he was born, ran a seasonal restaurant and guest house, but his greatest love and passion was the 'wildlife foundation' he set up and the 'wildlife symposium's' he organised each year. He was a caretaker of the Burren, of the wild animals and flowers, of the hills and the seas. Like ancient Indian shamans, his sacred journey, was to protect and honour that wild beautiful piece of the Earth and to draw people there, to bask in its ancient healing energies. He was a deeply spiritual man, attuned to and respectful of the divine energies of Mother Earth.

So, I went to the Hospital and seeing John in such a sterile intensive care environment (despite its good intentions), felt like watching a fish out of water or a dolphin in captivity. He belonged to the mountains and the seas, to his dog Elvis, to nature. He battled hard, insisted he was not dying, did not want to die and he was not consciously ready, for perhaps a week or two. John in many ways was a very private man and wanted us to get on with our lives. Being exposed, in a hospital bed, was difficult for him.

I went back to work for a time in Dublin and then to a weekend workshop in Co. Wicklow, about the 'Bush Flower Essences', facilitated by the Australian Ian White. As we sat in meditation on the Sunday morning, the psychic/emotional pull I felt, to leave and support John, was the strongest pull I ever experienced to go and be somewhere. With my Dad, it had been a dream that called me. Now, it was like a magnetic pull in every cell of my body. I knew, without being told, that John was dying and a huge force was pulling me. He was calling me and I knew that very clearly. The long drive was tough – having a very psychic energy that attunes to others so easily (especially when they are in need), at times I felt I was dying too. Many times I have been asked to support people in their process of birthing into the spirit world, like a spiritual midwife I guess.

That night, my cousin Caitriona and I sat with John (all of us Pisceans). It was his most difficult night and he struggled to breathe. In that space just before death, it is like watching someone in labour, as they prepare to birth themselves into their spirit home. The next evening I brought 'Transition essence' (made from Australian bush flowers) and 'Frankinsence massage cream' (a rite of passage cream) and asked John's permission to administer them, while explaining briefly what they were. My cousin Paula (another Piscean) and I sat with John as I massaged his feet and hands and I felt him begin to let go. The hands of his spirit family and guides were in mine as I massaged him and I felt deeply honoured to be gifted with the job of massaging him through that birth canal. Also I rubbed the 'transition essence' on his wrists and pulse points many times. All of these beautiful healing flowers were so compatible with his very essence.

He was very weak, hardly able to speak that night and before I left he tried to tell me something I could not understand and as I got up to leave, he roared 'reflexology' across the ward and there was no doubt, but that he wanted me to massage him again. I massaged his feet and hands and he was deeply asleep as I left to go home. His lips were blue and I knew it would not be long.

While tossing and turning in my bed unable to sleep, the phone rang and John was very close to death. As I drove to the hospital in the early hours of the morning, a big red fox jumped out in front of the car, causing me to jump on my brakes and as he ran to the other side, I knew John was gone. He had befriended a wild fox when he was younger and so he went back to the wild. He died at that time. As in shamanic Indian culture, he shape shifted into a fox as he left and so I got my goodbye and thank you. And thank you too John for trusting me and allowing me in, at that most vulnerable and final moment of your sacred journey in the Earth. My energy is shamanic. I put transformational journeys on tape for people all the time. All that I am writing here, I have never shared with my family as we don't communicate much about the invisible world, yet it is the very essence of who I am.

So Eileen and John, both in their sixties, the youngest members of my Mother's childhood family had gone and as a result the ancestral family home, on the shores of the Burren, would be reborn also. When someone close to us dies, it reflects something for us; a part of us is dying and being reborn also. We move more into the core of our own spiritual journey and selves and it is our job to process the emotions that surface so they can take us where we need to go, challenging and all as that might be. There is unlimited spiritual healing and support available to us. John was a 9th. March Piscean with a thirty three birth number, just like me and his death reflected a major change for me and my expression in the Earth.

The day I returned from the funeral, my son Kenn and his partner Celine, phoned to say they were expecting a baby and I was to be a grandmother for the first time. There was hope, a new life, a new beginning and I was ecstatic as I adore small children and have always felt that babies are divine and edible.

A month or so later, Lyn, the psychic visionary artist we had met in Australia, arrived in Ireland, as I had organised individual and group work for her in Dublin and Galway. The day she arrived in Galway, a phone call came from Kenn and Celine, to say they were expecting twins. There was much excitement and celebration and a feeling of being on a high. I participated in Lyn's last workshop and as I was drawing, I saw an image of what looked and felt like John, but then it changed into a woman with deep blue hair and eyes and as I looked around her heart area, there were two faint but clearly visible outlines of the twins.

In this art form, you are taught to look for the hidden images and then draw them to the surface. They are messages from spirit and the unconscious. Everyone in the group was as amazed as I was and Lyn coaxed the images to the surface, as I did not feel qualified enough to do so. I felt deeply emotional and could not speak through the entire development of this picture. The twins outline was white and they were surrounded by this clear deep blue but the colour at the outer edges of the picture was a mottled grey and I felt uncomfortable with it. I did not know at the time, that the woman spiritually holding (defined by the blue hair) the twins in the light was me.

Shortly afterwards, it was discovered that the twins were identical and they were experiencing a potentially dangerous uterine condition called 'twin to twin transfer syndrome'. They were connected by blood vessels where one was receiving too much blood and growing too fast, causing huge pressure on the heart and the other was receiving too little blood, was very tiny and pushed into a corner of the womb. There is no known cure for this syndrome, but a disconnection of the blood vessels, through foetal surgery, while having its risks, gives the babies a much better chance of survival. So this surgery was performed in the womb, by a pioneering foetal surgeon in Harley Street, London and it went well.

I knew the twins were in trouble, big trouble, even after this surgery and I constantly sent healing to them, as did many others, hoping for a miracle. I would wake up at night and feel myself holding the twins in a healing light. My last thought at night and first one in the morning and countless times during the day was to wrap them in light and love. After spending between twenty seven and twenty eight weeks in the womb, babies Katie and Nikki were born. I was a grandmother for the first time, excited, elated but also very worried, as things were on the edge with our little angels. They had to be revived after birth and were rushed to the neonatal unit in a Dublin maternity hospital, where they were placed on life support and every other possible intervention available.

Sometime after midnight, we, the family, were called to the hospital, as Katie was not doing well. I will never forget the first time I saw her. She was beautiful, perfect, a little miracle because she had battled so hard to be born, so brave and courageous and then I tiptoed to see Nikki and got a shock. Though identical, she was so tiny and her little body was so red, from all she had been through. They were courageous, angelic, tiny warriors, so beautiful, so perfect and so sick. I knew it would take a major miracle for them to survive and the possibility was if one went, the other would, as they were so connected.

I was so in love with my new grandchildren and I spoke to them quietly, through the glass walls of their incubators. The first words of a grandmother to her two beautiful grandchildren were, I love you, we would love you to stay, we want you both so much, but if you cannot, we will find a way to let you go. They say the greatest gift of love is letting go. This was a gift that was hard to give. The neonatal team were amazing, as they facilitated the arrival of the extended heartbroken family.

Some time later Katie died peacefully free of all tubes and monitors in the arms of her parents. As Katie was dying, Nikki began to go downhill and the team worked hard to stabilise her. After death, Katie looked like a peaceful sleeping baby.

Nikki had stabilised a bit and as we had missed a night's sleep, we went home to rest, but just as we drifted off to sleep, the phone rang and the nightmare began again. Nikki was going to join her sister. The medical team had worked tirelessly to save her, as they had with Katie, but there is a moment, when ethically and morally, the intervention must stop. Some time later, Nikki also died peacefully in the arms of her parents. My beautiful identical grandchildren were reunited and tucked up together in a cot, like two peaceful sleeping angels. They had gifted themselves to us for as long as they could, like exotic flowers, one day was their lifetime. They came with a gift for each of us and those gifts will unfold in our lives, little by little.

The twins other grandmother dressed Nikki and I dressed Katie, after the post mortem. It was an honour and a once in a lifetime experience to dress Katie, the only time I would ever dress and cuddle, my grandchild. Sometimes I think it is better, when we don't know, we are doing something for the last time. I felt nervous dressing Katie, afraid I would hurt her, ridiculous and all as that might sound and afterwards I held her in my arms. Her little mouth was opened and had moisture in it, like any other sleeping baby. I rocked her, talked to her and drank every fibre of her into my being. It was heartbreaking and beautiful all at the same time. There was never a good time to put her into the little white coffin, with Nikki, but eventually that time came. They were tucked up together, with their toys, teddies, books, bracelets (a gift from me) and all they could need to keep them happy, and a sea of people came to celebrate them and guide them on their way, to the next part of their journey.

It was heartbreaking to see my son carry that little white coffin into the church and I was haunted for some time by the coffin going into the Earth. The service and singing was beautiful, the priest cried and called the service a group hug, while the choir sang, 'Somewhere over the rainbow' and 'In the arms of the angels'.

I woke up crying each morning for quite a while and felt I could not release the twins, as I had held them in a spiritual healing light, for so long. During one night, when I was semi asleep, the daughter I miscarried, some twenty one years earlier, came for them and only then, could I release them. I cried my way right through that night. I have experienced many deaths in my life, but this has been the hardest. There are no nice memories of things you shared and did together. You feel cheated. There is nothing to hold onto. It is, a death that guides you into the very heart of your spiritual journey and while in Crete on holidays, where I began to write this book, I cried healing tears, as I watched grandmothers and parents, playing with their baby girls on the beach.

If the twins had lived, they may have had lots of physical challenges and somehow for me personally, I felt they represented an end to a pattern of sacrifice and holding me back from my need, to give myself full permission to write this book and express myself fully and completely in the Earth. I heard them speaking in my ear many times as I was sunbathing on the beach in Greece, where there was time and space, for me to grieve, beneath my sunglasses. So, sleep tight, fly free, rest in the arms of the angels my little grandchildren and thank you for touching me so deeply and for shining a light into the next part of my journey.

So these four deaths represented a spiritual gateway for me, a bridge to the future and a birth canal to the free expression of all I have gathered and experienced. Times of emotional intensity are times of initiation, times when we birth ourselves anew in the Earth, times when we step, into the depth of the sacred journey of our soul, on this Earth.

Chapter 13

The Heart of the Matter

Shortly after Katie and Nikki died, we left our western ocean side cottage and invested in a new home, in Co. Meath, quite close to the heart of Ireland. This home is situated in the fields of an ancient monastic settlement, where thousands of monastic students were educated and a vast body of sacred writing was said to have originated here. From this now silent seat of learning and divine writing, I have somehow been held, encouraged and supported to write about my own sacred journey, as it is here that I have written the vast majority of this book.

The processing of my grief and the writing of my story, intermingled, one fuelling the other. When it came to Katie and Nikki's first birthday, those that were available came for a celebration of them, where we lit candles in a bowl of sand, wore illuminated halos, held hands and listened to their music and sent our wishes and helium balloons heavenward. As we made an omelette afterwards, shivers ran up our spines as each and every egg, had a double yoke inside. Our heavenly angels found a way to say hello. My grief greatly eased after that.

My life settled into a new pattern of writing, working one week of the month in Galway city and the remainder of the time, from my home. Socially, I have taken great pleasure from the many meals and the endless laughter I have shared with family and friends. Over the last year and a half I have spent many pleasurable hours exploring the lakes and the oceans in the kayak, with my 'soulmate', and partaken in a myriad of different exercise forms, from walking and the gym to salsa dancing and swimming.

I was fast approaching my fiftieth birthday and I wanted to complete this book, as close to that date as was humanely possible. This book is a celebration of the first fifty years of my life and it has taken me that many years, to give myself permission, to fully express the centre or heart of who I am. Like the chicken breaking out of the egg, the flower opening out of its bud, or the bird spreading its wings, I, through this book and I hope many more books to follow, am giving myself full permission to express the full, true and honest voice of my heart in this World. It involved breaking through many layers of conditioning, expressing and letting go many deep emotions, old attitudes and fears and swimming through my being to sit at the very centre of my heart and soul, to listen to the truth of who I am.

The journey has been a precious and valuable one, that despite its many intense challenges, I would not change for the world. All the wisdom, knowledge and precious insights I have gathered, are worth their weight in gold. There is a quiet, unshakable confidence within me now and the satisfaction that I have honestly followed my star, clearing whatever was in the way, so I could shine the true light of my being into this World.

The weekend before my birthday in March 2006, I had a bad cold and flu like symptoms and though I was feeling unwell, I went out with my sister Marian, who has always been so loving and supportive of me, for a sisterly celebration. We shopped till I dropped, had a delightful lunch and I was bemused, as she acted out of character, ignoring my obvious exhaustion, cough and worn out façade, delaying taking me home at every opportunity. Day dreaming of my jamies and cosy bed, I finally said to her, I am exhausted, unwell and I just have to go home. That did not deter her from delaying me a little longer.

However, when we finally arrived at my home, all was quiet, until I opened the door of the living room and there before me, was a sea of faces, from every aspect of my life. I went into shock, unable to speak and totally confused I fixed my eyes on a dishy, embarrassed, Italian man, (who I had only met once), wondering who was he, did I know him, had I met him before? My mind was trying to catch up with what was happening and it was a few minutes, before I realised that this was a surprise birthday party for me. After greeting everyone and kissing this vast number of people, who filled three rooms in my home, I escaped upstairs to change my clothes and adjust to an evening of a very different colour, to the one I had planned.

My 'soulmate' had gathered an army of friends and family, to create an evening I would never forget. It was a tribal affair and no room or stone was left unturned, in the preparation of this celebration. I was guided to sit in a darkened room, on the sofa and with the tribe surrounding me, the television was switched on and a DVD of my life, lovingly and painstakingly put together by my 'soulmate', began to unfold. Accompanied by beautiful music, it zoomed in on my grandparent's homes, in the Burren of beautiful Co. Clare and the magical 'Cape Clear' island off the west Cork coastline. I was instantly overwhelmed by emotion, as this journey of picture and sound took me through my childhood, teenage years into adulthood, marriage, motherhood, friendships, holidays and the moments of now, incorporating almost everyone I ever knew. It was mind blowing, and I tried and failed miserably to control my tears of awe and memory. It is a beautiful gift I will treasure forever.

Then, I was guided into the kitchen to a spectacular table setting of a white linen tablecloth adorned with red, white and black feathers. At the centre sat a two tiered chocolate cake, covered in white icing, adorned with many feathers and a Venetian mask crowned the whole affair, in honour of my trip to Venice the following week, to celebrate my birthday. Beside the cake, there was an exquisite bouquet of flowers, with three pearls of wisdom threaded through green fronds, projecting out of this beautiful display. A chocolate fountain, dancing candles, love and friendship completed the kitchen vista. Another room contained a mouth watering selection of every possible type of food. There were balloons decorating every room and candles lighting everywhere. I was unable to eat for the first time in my life. I completely lost my appetite.

Next, I was called into the kitchen, where people had formed a human tunnel, for me to dance through, to 'Absolutely everybody', by Vanessa Amorosi. The tunnel felt like a birth canal and these people like the midwives that had come to birth me, into the next space of my life. Laughter and joy bubbled up inside me, the minute I entered the tunnel and it led me into the darkness of the garden, to a giant spiral of seaweed, wood bark and shells. I followed the spiral into the middle, where a magical hazel tree sat and lit a candle, to celebrate my life and make my wishes, from a torch at the centre.

Everyone followed, lighting candles, making their wishes and dropping them into hand painted glass jars, in a multitude of colours, until the giant spiral was dancing with lights. Next I was guided to a goddess throne that occupied the right hand corner of the garden. It was adorned with wings, a giant golden bow, a magical mirror, lots of jewels and pearl necklaces on a table to the right and a wishing fountain on the left. When I sat on the throne, my niece Rachel put a tiara on me and my friend Ben flicked a switch and the entire garden lit up. I roared with laughter. It felt like a magical fairy wonderland and I was a fairy child, in a magical mystical land. I felt incredibly happy in that garden that had been so lovingly created, to celebrate me. There was a freedom and abandonment in it, that took my breath away and I wanted to stay there forever.

In the left hand corner of the garden on an easel, was a newly framed picture of my spiritual guide Indi, who lovingly journeys with me through every day and my Indian rattle. There were two little fairies to represent Katie and Nikki, a large hand woven reindeer and a swan and torches were lighting everywhere. It had taken the tribe an entire day to create this magical wonderland. It was a freezing cold night and wrapped in coats and shawls I danced around the garden, with some friends. I made my future wishes before I left the garden.

I received an abundance of beautiful gifts and the surge of powerful love and friendship that was gifted to me that night, more than supported me, to birth myself, into the next part of my life. It felt like the biggest, most important birthday I have had, since I was born. So yes in everyway I felt I was being reborn and celebrated. There were more surprises to follow. Davin had made a DVD for me, with beautiful music, that focused more on my life as a mother and he gifted me a most beautiful, fully bound book entitled 'This is Your Life' – well half of it - The book contained a very moving introduction from him and personal wishes and acknowledgements from many people in my life. It also contained a tremendous number of photographs, with allocated space for me to write my memories. I was deeply moved by this gift and will treasure it always. I am deeply grateful for all I received from my 'soulmate', friends and family on that wonderful night. I don't think I came back to reality for a month.

So, the time has come to say goodbye and I am delighted that I have finished this, my first book and yet sad that the journey is over and the time has come, to let, yet another precious baby, fly the nest. In my life so far, there have been many challenges and there have been many wonderful moments. There have been many firsts when there was no one to show me the way and these times, taught me to go inside and seek my inner wisdom and to communicate with the heavenly beings that are guiding my pathway. I look forward to the future with hope in my heart and the knowledge that all we dream of is possible, in this beautiful Earth of ours.

My book is a gift to you of all that I am and may you know that just as I have travelled the journey, so can you. May you believe in yourself and find in your heart the freedom to spread your wings and fly.
Love always.

Tricia
21st. June 2006

Chapter 14

STORIES SHARED BY CLIENTS ABOUT THEIR INDIVIDUAL HEALING EXPERIENCES

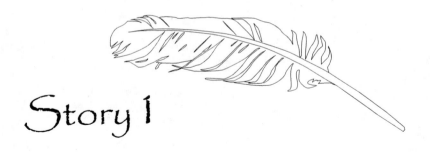

Story 1

Aoife's Story

I have been working with Tricia for over six months to date and the following words describe what it has been like for me – "a journey towards freedom, self development and happiness".

For years, I had a tendency to search for "something better", something I never clearly identified and I always looked for things outside of myself, in order to achieve fulfillment, never stopping or taking "quality time" to look within, and feel, and identify, what I really wanted, and what was best for me.

I went to see Tricia on the recommendation of a good friend and like all other "new things", I had embarked upon in my life, I went to my first appointment without giving it a lot of thought, not knowing what to expect and hoping that it would somehow enhance my life. I recall Tricia gently asking me at one stage, why I had come, and my reply being that I just wanted to be a better person. She explored this with me and after some time, the outcome both shocked and upset me. I talked and cried about an issue I thought I had "dealt" with years ago, one I never discussed, certainly not with strangers! The issue was abortion and I had been carrying guilt, anxiety, self doubt and regret, for years.

Tricia was open, non judgemental and kind. She listened and I felt safe. She tuned into those who were with me at that time, in what I describe as the "spirit world", and she described and explained various things to me. She then covered me in a blanket, placed her hands above my head and on my shoulders, at different times, whilst she did some healing and talked to me. She recorded this part of the session, so that I could take it home and listen to it. My homework involved writing to the baby, explaining many things and the associated feelings, then when I was ready, burning the letter and doing a ritual which I chose – i.e. burning the letter and planting it with some bulbs in the soil. It was a few weeks before I could do this. I cried a lot and listened to Tricia's tape many times during those weeks. I recall listening to the tape and somehow feeling safe and supported.

Since that first appointment, I have written many letters, to many different people and have performed quite a few similar rituals under Tricia's guidance. It has been a gradual process of letting go, which has enabled me to forgive and accept myself, and to free myself from the pain of guilt, self judgement and low expectations, of what I deserve. Other homework following healing sessions with Tricia involved – saying positive affirmations, writing what I want –e.g. my dreams for certain areas of my life and doing a collage with pictures representing the aspects of these dreams, writing a self appraisal and writing how I would ideally like to handle various situations in my life.

After each session with Tricia, I would come away feeling calm, supported and able to handle what life presents. During one particular session, I resisted Tricia's advice, saying that I could not possibly do this or that and I gave numerous reasons for my reluctance, to which she calmly listened and reiterated the importance for me of doing these particular things – yet I resisted. A week later I mysteriously realised that I had actually done the "this, that, the other and more".

I have changed over the past six months and the changes have been commented upon by many who know me. I laugh more. I am less stressed and more creative. I know what I want and what I will tolerate. I am clearer in my thinking and my thinking is much more positive than it ever was. I have basically lightened my load, shed the baggage and the negativity and realised what I need to do for myself. Amazing things happen as I clearly ask for what I want and for what is best for me and I receive. I have even got parking spaces in car parks, where there seemed to be no hope of ever getting a space.

I appreciate everything in my life and I give thanks regularly. I do frequent clear-outs of possessions, particularly clothing. I enjoy doing this and I have found that shortly after doing so I inevitable find in some shop, that nice top or pair of trousers I have wanted for ages. I prepare for the sessions I have with Tricia in so far as I do my homework and think about what I would like to ask her and what I would like her to help me with. I no longer drift along reacting to external forces.

The bulbs blossomed into an array of colourful flowers, that I have enjoyed seeing develop. When sewing the bulbs I was slightly anxious about how I would react once they would mature i.e. would I be upset? Would they be a reminder of the issue? Fortunately, what they became was something beautiful to look at, nothing more, other than a strong reassurance that I was doing well. Thank you Tricia - your gifts of healing, understanding, intuition, kindness and love have brought me and I am sure many others, to where I am now.

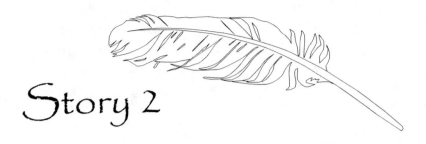

Story 2

Esther's Story

My name is Esther. I met Tricia in 1995. My brother had been killed in a car accident the previous year and I was heart broken. I went to meditation classes with Tricia for about ten weeks. I went to these classes to help me get through the sadness and upset that I felt at the time. I found the classes very helpful even though I ended up, on a few occasions, crying during the class. It helped me to deal with the feeling of loss. I remember Tricia saying after a class that she felt that my brother was with me during it. I was delighted and amazed, wishing I could see or feel him myself. Even though, the death of a loved one is a very sad, heart breaking experience, it showed me how to view it, in a more understanding way and I know that my brother is always there for me spiritually and looks after me each day.

My next meeting with Tricia was in the last year. I had a stress related illness. I came to see her feeling very stressed and anxious. I attended two healing sessions. I found the messages Tricia had for me, so accurate and portrayed exactly what was going on in my life at the time. She did beautiful healing meditations with me, mentioning my brother in it. I felt relaxed and calm during the meditation. I was able to take home the meditation tapes and listen to them. I played them on a daily or weekly basis, whichever I needed. I found by doing this, it helped me deal with emotions and become less stressed. I started to feel a sense of relaxation within myself and a feeling of being at peace.

I also attended an Xmas meditation evening last December, where I did a few different kinds of meditations. They were absolutely beautiful. I found I was totally calm, relaxed and tuned into them. My mind and body felt totally relaxed and recharged afterwards.

In my opinion, Tricia is an Earth Angel sent here to do beautiful healing work. She is always helpful and has supported me, at difficult times in my life and brought me to a much better understanding of myself. One sentence I remember from a healing session is – "we are never, where we are not meant to be in this life journey". That one sentence has let me view things in a different more positive light. Her work is wonderful and was a life saver for me when I needed it.

Story 3

Linda's Story

I have been having healing sessions with Tricia Sheehan for two years and I am now going to attempt to put into words, the effect this remarkable woman has had on my life.

When I met Tricia Sheehan, I had reached a turning point in my life. I had moved from London to Ireland, split up from my relationship, which left me devastated and I was also battling with a serious weight problem. I was deeply unhappy with myself and my life. I was at my lowest ebb and had no real sense of inner worth.

I simply cannot explain to you how grateful I am to have met Tricia Sheehan and how much I value and respect the important work that she carries out, to the highest integrity.

Through her healing sessions and beautiful personalized

meditative journeys, which she puts on tapes, marked "Merlin moments", she taps into exactly what you need to know at that time, to make every moment of your life, one of great happiness, contentment and peace. She immediately recognised the great sensitivity I possess and taught me, it is something to cherish and not detest. She is able to access your emotional space and jump straight to the heart of the matter. She has taught me that the dreams and desires I have are not just impossible pipe dreams, but very real and attainable realities.

I encouraged, Tricia Sheehan, to write her book "Sacred Journey of a Celtic Visionary", so that she can reach the widest possible audience. My wish is that other people will know, understand and perhaps be lucky enough to experience what Tricia Sheehan's magical sessions and gifts are all about.

I urged her to write this book to help you (like she has helped me) create the kind of life that works and makes sense, and most importantly, a life you are living and truly loving, as the powerful, fulfilled person, you have always wanted to be.

The work Tricia Sheehan does creates true freedom in your soul. In her book, this glamorous, non-judgemental healer with the utmost compassion and sensitivity leads us on a path to something every one of us seeks in our heart – inner joy. With her innate abilities and wicked sense of humour, Tricia introduces us to techniques that enable us to discover, our own state of true inner joy and acceptance – the kind that saints and mystics have written about throughout the ages. She helps us to build a centre of emotional and spiritual self reliance on the inside, a centre that will allow you to live everyday with greater joy, greater strength and the peace in your heart to know that you are good enough, just because you are here on the earth plane, and that it is your divine right to be loved, treasured and respected.

Most of all, my sessions with Tricia Sheehan and the many magical "Merlin moments" we have shared together, have given me the feeling of true freedom – the freedom that comes from finding a source of security and happiness inside yourself – happiness that nothing and no-one can ever take away from you and the self confidence to finally face my fears.

Tricia Sheehan has helped me in so many ways. She has helped me to understand difficult family dynamics and unravel my childhood issues that have brought me to where I am today.

This modest lady takes no credit for the success and happiness I find in my life today. That said, without hesitation, I urge you to read her book "Sacred Journey of a Celtic Visionary", so you may too find inspiration, from this amazing healer and visionary.

I ask you sincerely to please support her important work. I can honestly say I owe a great deal of gratitude to Tricia Sheehan and her work. My life would not be the beautiful journey it now is, if it was not for this true light worker. I am blessed to have met her and I know you will be touched by her story, as much as I am.

Sincerely,

Linda Duncan 2006

Working with Tricia Sheehan

Anne's Story

It is a joy to write about working with Trish (albeit a struggle for me to do justice to her work and to describe succinctly and concretely what she does), because it was uplifting to work with her and one unique outcome has been the birth and arrival of my baby girl Grace. Indeed it was exactly this time (Solstice June '05) that I found out I was pregnant, a news of unexpected and great joy.

I can but give a glimpse into what it has meant for me to work with Trish, and as my story will explain later, at a particularly significant and indeed life changing time for me.

I have been very lucky to have met with and worked with Trish. She has been a hugely positive, affirming, supportive, caring force in my life.

Birth and birthing both in its symbolic and physical manifestations have been the dominant themes in my work with her so far. And indeed Trish was a mid-wife in every way, apart from her physical presence at the time of delivery!

So too, as in any birthing process, healing with Trish is a collaborative venture. She enables one to restore and reclaim one's wisdom, ones deep knowing, one's higher or true self.

Of course, we all tend "to go for healing" at times of crisis, of illness, of dis-ease, with self and others. I, too, am no exception to this. But in a session with Trish, when the difficulties, crisis, issues or 'stuff' presenting themselves, are put out and uncovered, to see what the patterns or emotional content underpinning them are, the potential for transformation, for release, for finding one's own healing power can evolve. Trish certainly seeks out, inspires and brings forth the healer in her client also. When this happens, waves of relief, of deep knowing, of energy, of life force are released (tapped into), and this is the point of joy, a joy which is both, real and present, yet effusive and fleeting. We seemingly (or most of us) don't have the ability to contain or hold joy for long. Yet it is the memory of those freeing – joy filled moments in healing sessions with Trish, that remind me of the power of these sessions and of healing which inspires me, to recommend this and Trish to others.

Trish, as a healer, can be gentle, extremely empathetic and compassionate, but she is also direct and challenging. For all of us, the crises, conflicts, dramas and stories of our experiences, reflects our relationships and difficulties with others. Trish enables one to see these dramas as aspects of one's own patterns, struggles, projections and as the "raw material" of the self, which needs to be owned, integrated, taking responsibility for what one has attracted, or engaged with, to define more clearly "my stuff", my needs as distinct from that of others. It can take time to take responsibility for one's responses and actions. Working with Trish ensures clearer insights into the core issues of one's soul story, and in conversation with one self, one's true essence and guides, inspires an "ah-ah" moment – i.e. this is what is happening here.

She also enables and encourages one to trust one's process. It is important to say she is non-judgmental. If one is struggling to hear what is being said or to accept something, she will work with it, so that one can find one's truth, one's strength, one's wisdom, one's ease, in order that change and healing can happen.

I find the naming, structure and components of her sessions as having meaning at many levels. This meaning is both symbolic of and actual to the process of healing.

The Sessions

The name 'White Feather' healing, the naming of the sessions on the tape as "Merlin moments", the drinking of the cup (as in Australian Bush essences) and their affirmations, for me enact the healing process. And together with the healing part of the session (on the plinth with a recording of what Trish says), imbue a magical sense to the sessions and indeed offer a metaphor for understanding healing itself. There is an aliveness, a fluency, a congruency between all the components of each session, which I love and adds much to the overall, each complete in itself, yet finds resonance in the whole.

My Story

I began to work with Trish after the last of three miscarriages in March 2004. I had been working with others and Anne Campbell, most regularly of all, in this period 2001-2004, and with Anne and Trish concurrently '04 to Feb '06, along with other medical and spiritual expertise. Interestingly, there was always a consistency in this work between the different healers and that too had its own power to affirm and trust, in what is right for me and at the right time.

I instinctively knew that it would be a good idea to work with Trish after the third miscarriage. I needed to find out and explore what was going on here. So much unfolded during those sessions and in complementary sessions with Anne, I can but focus on a few key themes.

The Pre-pregnancy time

I had about 15 sessions with Trish in the pre-pregnancy period. The work of this period could be characterised by a journey, a coming home to a self, a giving birth to myself, my needs, my truth, being at ease in my own skin. This I was somewhat unprepared for, as I was so focused on the dream of another child, for me, for our relationship as a couple and also to give my older girl a sibling, but we were losing sight of the dream. Trish instilled positivity and encouragement. The dream of giving birth to another child was connected to a giving birth to myself. This work was tough. I so wanted it all to happen now and I still remember the angst when Trish was beseeching me to give it time – a year. Paradoxically the process was about allowing the dream, give birth to me. There are many areas that come up for exploration in the coming home to oneself, suffice to name here the patterns of thinking and emotions that needed to sit easily with me :-

-       that I am good enough as I am
-       that I am worthy of this
-       that I deserve this

So too, trust and trusting my process, my body, the creative process and my ability to create, were at the core of this healing work and my struggles. Images, body-wisdom, memories, stories, bush remedies and healing – visualisation and meditative journeying were part of these sessions. Ritual too had a role and capacity to heal. One such ritual focused on grieving and letting go :-

A Timing

Oct 1st. '04   An ultrasound photo of last pregnancy fell

out of my diary in session with Trish.
We explored not letting go.

Oct 3rd.'04   I had a wee ritual of burying the photo
and some ribbon, symbolic of previous
pregnancies and miscarriage.

Oct15th.'04   My friends baby was born. My babe was
due at this time. The day after I was
broken hearted and could not stop crying.

Oct17th.'04   My friend Bernadette's months memorial -
again a focus for grieving.

Oct 23rd.'04   The funeral mass and burial of Trish's
grandchildren, became both a focus
of grief and a time of healing for me.

The Womb Journey

I discovered that I was pregnant on summer solstice
'05. Trish worked with me throughout the pregnancy
journey. I became pregnant with the assistance of natural
procreative technology and the power of prayer, healing,
medical expertise and the positive energies of many. It was
a time of great anxiety with specific episodes, where the
pregnancy was threatened with loss.

Trish's weekly sessions in the early month or two kept me
calm, positive and focused. The thrust of these are summed
up by the affirmations critical to this journey :-

"I trust my body"
"I trust my womb"
"I trust my baby's sacred journey"

I loved these sessions, particularly the tapes of the healing journeys, which I played and re-played (and fell asleep to) between sessions. Deep patterns of fear kept coming up. The tapes and these healing sessions were a critical focus in my ability, to believe in this pregnancy, the child's journey along with the medical intervention. The healing work touches and stills the heart. A great sign of this work was the look in baby Grace's face when she heard Trish's voice in person, at about a month old. Two of the text messages Trish sent me, just prior to the birth illustrate her level of care and support.

"The hands of the guides will be guiding birth of babe and it will happen only when the moment is right". – Feb 8th. 2006

Love, light, hugs, kisses, miracles, magic – enjoy the wonder of your deepest dream. May a host of angels sing to ye, as the baby is born and may you feel safe and present". – Feb 11th. 2006 (2 hours prior to birth – 9am). "

And I was present as Grace was born on Feb 11th. 2006. The womb journey, her birth and even since then it is, quite amazing, in the sense of accepting ones dream coming true …!

Trish assisted, mid-wived the birth of this dream and both she and her work were a total gift to me and my family, which we can never forget.

Working with Tricia Sheehan

Kathleen's Story

When I first met Tricia in 2000 I was an emotional and physical wreck. I had come through a very acrimonious marriage break-up and was left with five children – one who has a terminal illness. I was also in severe financial difficulties; my confidence was at an all time low and my life was going nowhere.

In June 1999 I decided to sell my house to relieve the financial pressure. I had found a smaller one which I liked and I would be able to buy it with the proceeds from the sale and have some money left over. A year later, I still had not managed to sell my house, even though it was a boom time and all the houses around me, were selling within weeks of going on the market. It was then that Tricia found me and she continues to find me every time I need her. I didn't go looking for her – I rang the centre where she worked, looking for another therapist I had visited before. Tricia answered the phone and told me the other lady didn't work there anymore, but she could help me.

I was very sceptical of spiritual healing, even though I knew nothing about it, but I was so desperate I decided to try it and I'm very glad I did, because my life has changed completely.

I had two visits with Tricia, one at the end of June and one a week later. She helped me get rid of all the baggage that was holding me back. Within two months of my first session with her, I had sold my house and bought a much nicer one, than the one I had lost the previous year. Everything started to go well for me, from then on.

I was so amazed at her healing power that I immediately rang a close relative of mine, who had been going through a very traumatic time for the previous two years. This lady never ever answered the phone to anyone, but that day when I phoned her, she did answer. She told me afterwards that she was so low at that point, that she couldn't have gone on, for much longer. She visited Tricia and she has her own amazing story to tell, about her experience. I have recommended Tricia to a lot of people and those who have visited her all have had very positive experiences.

When I moved to my new house everything went well for me. I had no more money problems and my sick child went through a very healthy period. I heard Tricia had gone abroad and I didn't hear anything more about her for a few years – until I needed her again.

In 2004 my child became very ill and was hospitalised for a while, but recovered well. Then in 2005 she was hospitalised again and wasn't expected to live. She did pull through again, but I was finding it very difficult to come to terms with the prospect of her death and I was becoming very depressed. Out of the blue, I got a schedule of upcoming events from Tricia, in the post. I didn't even know she was back from her travels. At this stage, I had lost her address and phone number but now when I needed it, it was literally on my doormat. Needless to say, I got in touch and again the results of one session were amazing. A year and a half later, my child is still going strong and so am I!!

I don't know what happens when I go into that room with Tricia, but I always come away feeling re-energised and rejuvenated. She always has practical advice to give, but what I love most is that I don't have to do any of the work. She gives a relaxing enjoyable meditation, which does all the work and I just lie back and listen.

I feel and I know that there is a connection between us. Every time I need her, she turns up without me having to look for her. Even as I write this, there has been a 'mini crisis', which I am dealing with very well and Tricia has turned up again, in the form of a text message. This has happened on a number of occasions. It's as if she is reminding me that I am not alone, no need to panic, there is help out there.

I am convinced that someone in the spirit world is helping me, but there are times, when they cannot get through to me and that is when they use Tricia, to get through to me. It's a great feeling to know you are not alone and Tricia is always there to help, when the going gets too tough.

There are times when I feel like having a session with her, even when there is nothing wrong, because just being in her presence is a wonderful experience.

Working with Tricia Sheehan

Sinead Says....

Tricia has a rare talent of reflecting back the truth of a person's feelings. In articulating the emotions, she enables us to open our spirit to healing and allow divine energy to flow.

Her meditations resonate deeply and continue to gently guide and heal, long after the session is over.

A Time to be Born

Just before I succumb to the world of 'digital printing', I want to announce the arrival of baby Cian and baby Ella, my beautiful new heaven kissed grandchildren, who are 8 weeks old today. Mum, Dad, Richelle and the twins are doing well and Nana 'T' is very proud.

1st October 2006

Healing Examples

In the healing examples given, the names and personal details of clients have been changed to protect their identities.

ISBN 142510975-6

9 781425 109752